D1490975

WINETASTER'S
SECRETS

WINETASTER'S
SECRETS
ANDREW SHARP

STERLING
PUBLISHING CO., INC.   NEW YORK

Design: Images Creative Services, Toronto
Cover Photograph: Rolf Heinecke

ISBN 0-919157-14-9

Sterling Publishing Co., Inc.
Two Park Avenue
New York, N.Y. 10016

Acknowledgments

No book is a singular effort. "Winetasters Secrets" is not an exception. From all those learned wine lovers who provided the foundation for such a book, to my wife who typeset and proofed the material (and kept my spirits elevated), to a photographer named Lovello who produced photos on a moments notice, to those who willingly made certain photographs available, and finally to a publisher who understood the need for a work such as this — my gratitude is unreservedly extended.

And may I never overlook all those wine lovers who will purchase a copy of Winetasters Secrets — to them my creditors extend their gratitude.

Table of Contents

Preface

Only two ounces of the red liquid is poured. The man lifts his glass to eye level and studies it closely. As if some inaudible message had been received the glass is replaced on the starched, white linen table-cloth and a few notes are hastily scratched on the paper in front of him.

Again, the glass is elevated but this time he swirls the liquid round and round. Even before it has settled down his nose is thrust well into the glass and his body swells as he inhales deeply.

More notes are hurriedly added to the paper. He stops, returns his nose to the glass, sets it down once more, adding more cryptic scrib-bles to his growing chronicle.

At long last the glass reaches his lips. A small sip is taken, followed by an odd gurgling sound. A pause . . . and as if something had offended him he dispells the liquid into a nearby container.

Sitting back in his chair now, a pensive, quizzical look crosses his face. Leaning forward more notes are penned. And he passes on to the next glass.

A professional winetaster is at work.

And he does his job well . . . very well, indeed. In fact he's so pro-ficient his tolerance for error — when evaluating wines on a one hundred point scale — is less than three points on the average.

The *secrets* of that wine, its nature, revealed themselves quite easily to his trained palate. In a matter of minutes our taster has accurately determined the true quality of the wine and can advise wisely on its purchase. He knows where it ranks, its stature, in the wonderful world of wines.

But, most of us drink wine. Can we ever be as certain about the wines we drink? Or, are the secrets, those so-called mysterious talents of the winetaster so abstruse we must all be content with being barely more than spectators in this respect, forever passing from wine to wine, never knowing whether one is really better than another?

Can we ever learn how to judge wine quality with any degree of accuracy? One man, writing to a wine columnist expressed his frustration rather eloquently.

"*. . .ten years and ten wine books later I still don't know. Oh, I can pinpoint on a map all the classic wine regions and discuss first-hand a number of little wine villages I've visited in France and Italy. I can translate all the "winesse" on the labels of French, German and Italian wines and I've memorized several vintage charts and their ratings . . . but I still can't tell you, except in the most fundamental terms, whether one wine is really superior to another.*"

This winelover's plight is hardly unique or surprising for there is precious little wine information that deals precisely with the **KEYS** to tasting wine . . . in simple language *HOW TO.*

Oh yes, all those impressive "coffee table" wine books describe in eloquent and pictorial language the quaint history and customs of the famed winelands, which wine to serve with certain foods, their personal views of innumerable wines, etc., etc.

Yet, with the rarest of exceptions the **HOW** and **WHY** of winetasting is glossed over as if the author had reached a sensitive, restricted area clearly marked *"For Professionals Only".*

"Winetasters Secrets" focuses on this very facet of wine. Step-by-step this book reveals how it's done, how the experts, and now you, can determine, evaluate wine quality. It does so in a manner that neither simplifies nor complicates the subject.

The objective of this book then, is three-fold . . .

1) to encourage you to expand the use of your natural senses, increasing your enjoyment of all wine,

2) to help you develop the ability to judge consistently and accurately the quality of wines, for yourself,

3) to help you appreciate the differences in **qualitative** and **nonqualitative** wine characteristics.

But . . .

Introduction

TASTE is a funny thing! Not *ha ha* funny, peculiar funny. Even the definition of the word is a little confusing. It's both a verb and a noun. It means to eat or to drink; to have or to get experience; a manner or style.

You can describe your appreciation for fine literature, an operetta and a hamburger with the same word — **taste**. That's the confusing latitude the English language permits at times. So we're forced to address ourselves to this word from several different aspects, if we're ever to understand how it applies to wine and our ability to determine wine quality.

Much of the confusion appears when you try to describe the taste of something to someone else. In this situation taste is too often expressed as a very individual, subjective judgment . . . "I like it" or "I don't like it."

In a manner this introduces us to the first stumbling block to your being able to judge wine quality accurately — your personal taste, your likes and dislikes, in other words. They have very little to do with assessing the inherent, intrinsic quality or stature of a wine. Oh, I know you've been told so often the *best* wine is the one you like and you're probably asking yourself, "aren't I supposed to drink the wines I personally like?"

Certainly you are! That's only natural.

But your personal likes and dislikes are not the objective standards by which wine can accurately be judged. Some persons simply don't like wine at all. Are their tastes sufficient reason to discount all wines as worthwhile beverages?

Hardly!

However, even as one who enjoys wine your individual preferences may not coincide with the wines the so-called *experts* judge as being

11

fine or **great**. In fact, they may rate your choices quite inferior by comparison.

What then?

Should you switch brands? Should the judgments of the experts dictate your wine selections instead of your own tastes?

Never!

How foolish, and at times pretentious, to allow your own taste to be dominated by someone else's, even that of an expert. That's when taste becomes *taste* in a very artificial way.

"So what's the point? First you tell me my personal likes and dislikes are not the standards by which wine quality can be judged, then you tell me keep drinking the wines I like."

Confusing? Not really!

The point is simply this: your *taste*, as the word describes your individual likes and dislikes, is not static. It invariably changes, and is therefore something less than a dependable judge of the true, intrinsic quality of wine. This is often the difference between a professional and a novice winetaster, even a good amateur. The professional is able to set aside his personal preferences and judge the wine on its inherent merits, or lack of them.

You see, your taste is largely, if not completely, a learned experience, an acquired characteristic. So it's obvious a little experience and experimentation can alter your likes and dislikes considerably.

Your present taste for wine, or any substance for that matter, simply indicates your sense of appreciation at this particular moment. Consequently, if your wine knowledge and experience grow together so will your ability to discern wine quality. To ever increasing degrees you will become more sensitive to the qualities which characterize genuinely **fine** and **great** wines from those more **ordinary** in nature.

And these qualities are real, not contrived. They stamp each wine with a fundamental character or stature that does not depend on the rather fickle intricacies of anyone's personal likes or dislikes. I repeat — drink the wines you personally enjoy — but permit that joy to grow through education and experience. Under these tutors you'll begin to appreciate the **HOW** and **WHY** of wine quality.

To further illustrate let me use the very old but very graphic example of the **"apple and orange"** comparison. For those who are still convinced it's all a matter of personal taste . . . this helps.

Imagine sitting in front of you on a table a perfect, luscious, juicy Navel orange and beside it a sparkling, garnet red Delicious apple. Which is better, the apple or the orange? Or, is that a fair question? Most will respond negatively — no, it's not a fair question — you can't compare an apple with an orange, they're different. However, before you make your final decision consider this scenario.

In front of you now is again that perfect, juicy, Navel orange but this time the apple is not quite so appealing — it's still partially green with several obvious blemishes and bruises. When you bite into it you find it pulpy and lacking the crispness it should have. Now, I ask that same question — which is better the apple or the orange? It's obvious the orange is superior, for specific reasons . . . the apple possessing certain faults.

Reversing the situation, using a poor, dried-out orange compared to a perfect apple gives you the same example. So, now think of the things that are common to the apple and orange, that account for their quality. Both should be free of blemishes, both should have good color (albeit different colors), both should have a good fruit texture, pleasing levels of juiciness, a nice acid/sugar balance, and so on.

So, you **can** compare apples and oranges — when they are less than perfect . . . but only when you compare the truly qualitative factors, not the elements, the essences that differentiate an apple from an orange. When both are perfect, indeed it is a matter of individual preference, which you like best, or, which is *better* to you.

The same is true for wine. Less than perfect (I haven't seen too many perfect wines around lately) and you can compare them . . . evaluating one as superior to the other for specific qualitative reasons. Of course, you may still prefer a second-rate orange to the world's greatest apple but objectively you should realize the poor orange is of lesser quality than that perfect apple.

We can rightfully conclude then, wines have both **qualitative** factors which can be evaluated and compared as well as factors which are **non-qualitative**, but simply identify a *style* or *personality* and cannot be assessed as being superior or inferior, just different.

And the first real key is experience. Despite the lofty intentions of this book no author can precisely relate to you all the subtle differences between wines. You must experience for yourself the essence, the nature of each wine for itself. Then, with a bit of guidance, discipline and objectivity, the type these few pages hope to assist you with, you will begin to appreciate these differences far more easily and consistently than ever before. No matter how literate or ingenius the author, the written word can only go so far, providing a sort of condensed version of the real thing. The re-constituting agent is the personal experience you must add.

But this is often the opposite of a rather disconcerting trend. Too often new winedrinkers these days pick a favorite wine and tend to stick to it like a brand of beer or whiskey. This may please immensely the fortunate producer but it does little for your wine education. And please don't view the word *education* as I use it here, in its traditional context. Wine is one form of education you not only benefit from ultimately but you enjoy the learning process every bit as much.

By limiting yourself to a favorite wine, or even several, you sell yourself considerably short when it comes to experiencing your share of the infinite pleasures of wine. There are considerably more than 200,000 wine labels floating around the world market today. Besides, your favorite, if it is a better wine, will probably change from vintage to vintage whether you change brands or not.

Now, this doesn't mean you won't discover a number of labels you'll come to depend on for *everyday* use. Just don't stop there! Keep on experimenting. Your appreciation of wine quality, will never grow without such experience.

One goal of this small book then, is to help you develop an **objective** sense of taste as it pertains to wine; to assist you in a fundamental way to learn how you can evaluate and judge wine quality accurately, much the way professionals do. In other words, to focus on the keys winetasters use to unlock the secrets of any wine.

The benefit — a better understanding and greater enjoyment from all wine. The bonus — money. The money you'll save by learning to become a *wine* drinker instead of a *label* drinker.

I must temper this by adding, it is not my goal, with this book, to swell the ranks of professional winetasters, those who are qualified to sit on a panel of experts and critically analyze such things as Claret and Burgundy vintages. Such a skill, an art really, comes from years of experience and training in an environment no author could re-create with just the written word. But, being able to judge between the good, the bad and the undrinkable is well within the grasp of every winelover . . . with just a little help from a friend.

However, much of the literature available to guide budding *oenophiles* (winelovers) too often comes across as either somewhat *elitist* and dogmatic (the pronouncement from on high to the unwashed masses approach) or *anarchistic* (the do your own thing, totally promiscuous approach).

Winetasters Secrets charts what I hope is a very balanced, down-to-earth course. If this little work can add to both your knowledge and enjoyment of all well-made, honest wines it will have accomplished its purpose.

To establish and maintain this degree of objectivity and consistency I've been advocating there is need for a dependable pattern or guide. This guide should prompt or induce you to evaluate each wine in a consistently fair and objective manner. In other words a consistent evaluation *system* is needed. There are almost as many wine evaluation systems (see pages 93-99) in use today as there are winetasters. It is not an objective of this book to select or promote one as superior to any other. However, our human senses do impose upon us (if we choose to follow them) a natural sequence of events for the "sensory evaluation of wine." A good system should follow this course and take into consideration only these elements.

If we then consistently apply only these *objective, qualitative* factors the true intrinsic merit of each wine you taste should become quite apparent. As well as identifying the stature of the wine you will also be able to relate this to current pricing and determine for yourself whether the wine you're tasting is a bargain, just fair value for money, or you've been had by another slick commercial, misguided friend or artistic wine label.

Again, this all *may* have little to do with your liking the wine. There are a number of wines I enjoy immensely however, I do not delude myself into thinking that that makes them anything more than what some of them are, simple, ordinary wines. It just so happens they have a nature I enjoy but when evaluating them professionally I must be objective, rating them for what they really are.

After all, since you probably purchase wines to serve others, whether it's for family use or for some special business or social occasion; you should be able to step beyond personal tastes and competently judge wines that may not appeal to you specifically.

Although we will touch ever so briefly on other types of wine — dessert and sparkling — our primary concern will be the multi-purpose table wines — red, white and rosé.

This small work, though, does not pretend to be a winetasting party guide. It does not elaborate on the traditional hints about table settings, the number and arrangement of glasses, the bread vs cracker vs cheese debate, tasting sequences, how to be the ideal host or hostess, or wine and food matches* and so on. The focus is specifically on helping you learn HOW to judge wine quality and WHY wines differ.

Shall we proceed. . .

*See page 122

The Tastevin – generally considered a "Burgundian" tasting device is rooted in wine history. As far back as three centuries B.C. Greek wine lovers used a shallow metal cup to taste and sample wines.

Tools of the Trade 1

Before we get into the actual assessment of wine qualities it would be wise for us to consider briefly what it is you're going to employ to make those evaluations. Figuratively speaking, they are — *tools of the trade.* But you don't have to rush out and invest a lot of money to equip yourself with them. Chances are you have most of them already. Granted, they'll be found in more or less functional condition, depending upon the shape of the individual.

These most vital keys or tools of the wine trade are, of course, four of the basic human senses — **sight, smell, touch,** and **taste.** When liberally mixed with that sixth sense, *common* sense, much of the mystery and mystique surrounding wine quality quickly evaporates.

Unlike some rather imaginative writers, we'll overlook our fifth sense, that of **hearing,** as part of our wine judging equipment. The suggestion that the sound of fine wine cascading into an elegant glass is one of the true pleasures of wine, stretches even my liberal imagination.

Although, such sounds have admittedly been known to command my instant attention I don't think even the best wine judge could differentiate between the splash of stale coffee and that of fine wine. And as far as the scintillating fizz of a sparkling wine? Well, what about the Champagne of Ginger Ales and its fizz?

In a negative sense, however, music and extraneous sounds, like crowd noises, can produce predictable variations in your wine judging. Even well meaning comments about the wine can affect the objectivity of other tasters.

Without trying to create a sanctimonious silence, at least a few minutes of **Quiet Please!** is in order when tasting in a more serious vein.

Now, to the tools.

SIGHT

To start at the bottom and work upwards is not an unreasonable sequence of events. And so we shall. **Sight** is at the bottom of your senses in that it is the least perceptive of the four senses you'll employ. Your nose is the most precise, exacting sensory device you possess, far surpassing the rather coarse abilities of those two ocular outlets.

Besides, your eyes too often see only what you want them to see. That's where some of the problems originate. Despite the fact that each human eye has 130 million light receivers it's the brain that appraises or evaluates the picture transmitted to it. More than occasionally the brain details greater or lesser reality than what is actually there to see.

Appearance and **color** are the two major factors to be determined visually. However, that's considerably easier to say than to do.

To intimate that sight is the sense most easily, shall we say, *led astray*, would not be out of place. Just consider what can happen to your assessment of wine colors as influenced by the prevailing light.

Using common fluorescent tubes — as your major source of light — causes white wines to appear more *brilliant* or *clear* than they really are. The tendency under this light will be to consistently judge a white wine as being more yellow, while reds seem to be less red than in reality. Incandescent lighting (your everyday 60 watt bulbs and so on) has much the same effect but not quite so pronounced.

Strong indirect natural lighting is preferred and clear uncolored bulbs place second, as an artificial source of light. But not even natural lighting is problem free. There are factors with natural lighting that must be taken into consideration in using it to judge wine coloring. On cloudy days whites show up more yellow while reds appear more intense. And against a brilliant blue sky red wines display an unnatural brownish tinge.

A solid white background can be achieved. Rear lighting can also be used.

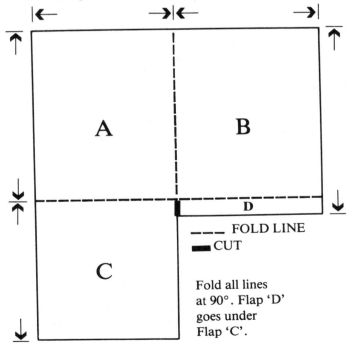

A

B

D

C

- - - - FOLD LINE
▬▬ CUT

Fold all lines
at 90°. Flap 'D'
goes under
Flap 'C'.

With so many lighting pitfalls you occasionally wonder if the wine expression *blind tasting* shouldn't really mean tasting blindfolded. Don't worry though, that's not likely to become a trend. Some wine experts have even mistaken a red for a white under such truly deprived circumstances.

Background coloring can also be a nuisance. While indispensable to the interior decorating trade these color influences can play havoc when you're trying to correctly assess wine colors. This type of distraction can come from walls, large pieces of furniture, lamp shades, carpeting, draperies and any number of colorful objects in close proximity to your wine glass. Keep in mind, a wine glass reflects images on its 360° circumference. So, if you're wearing a bright yellow tie or a vivid green blouse, guess what color will reflect in your glass.

Red lighting or a strong red reflection tends to make wine appear more brilliant, clear. Yellow causes white wines to shift noticeably towards a deeper shade of yellow as reds under this influence also become darker. Under a green influence little affect is noticeable on white wines but reds take on darker hues. Blue has the least abherrent influence and relatively accurate assessments can be made under this shade of lighting, with only a slight browning of red colors.

Your objective should be to assess wine colors under conditions that are as consistent as possible, not optimum. A simple *tent* as seen on page 21 can provide you with the consistency of background you need. and can be constructed easily, with little cost. This, of course, is for use in your more serious evaluations. Carrying it around to more casual samplings may create for you a reputation you may not particularly desire.

We could go on and on cataloguing the various influences that can affect our visual judgments but I think you get the picture by now. **Sight** gives us clues to the character of the wine, a sneak preview if you will. Our anticipation of the wine can be led off in various directions, good and bad, by how well and accurately we take advantage of our visual talents. So, sight is a key factor for which each wine judge, professional or amateur, must make considerable allowance. There is need to make these visual evaluations under as consistent conditions as possible, recognizing what various environmental influences can do.

SMELL

Phew!!

Most of us have had more than one occasion to personally express that qualitative opinion. It may have been a totally individual sentiment or one shared by most persons when confronted by particular smells. Some smells are like that . . . universally disagreeable. Whichever the case, propriety prevents me from elaborating on the more graphic examples of this type of odor.

But what is it that actually happens to cause this curious function of smell? It can repulse you totally or start you smacking your lips in anxious anticipation of a taste delight.

A small yellow patch approximately three sixteenths of an inch square, in the upper passage of the nose, does it all. From this moist, mucus covered patch two **olfactory** (smelling) nerves lead to what are called olfactory bulbs positioned approximately at the base of the brain. From this point impulses travel to the brain where they are interpreted as a distinct smell.

A little clinical as a description, agreed. But understanding how the old *snoze* works will help us appreciate just how vital it is to wine judging and enjoyment.

For anything to have a smell it must be, to a degree, volatile (easily vaporized). Its molecules must readily dissolve in that mucus covering the olfactory region and be strong enough to activate the nerve endings.

Earlier I suggested the nose was significantly superior to all other senses. How much superior? Some *nose* experts claim this most extraordinarily sensitive human device is several hundred times more sensitive to odors than your tongue is to tastes. Now that's superior! Perhaps you can begin to appreciate the role your little proboscis plays, or should play, in improving your wine judging abilities. I still claim Jimmy Durante could have been the world's greatest wine judge.

Another important factor to keep in mind, while we're still at the nose in our anatomical travels, is the dual manner in which we smell — in a sense, frontwards and backwards. When we breathe in, inhale, air passes over the olfactory region and we smell something, hopefully. However, when we take something into the mouth the odor of this substance again passes the olfactory region when we *exhale*, odors

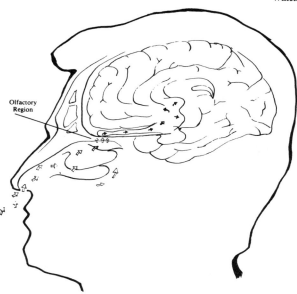

Olfactory
Region

OLFACTORY — Your ability to smell depends entirely on the tiny olfactory patch.

coming up the *back way*, so to speak. And most often this will be a superior way to smell. This is due primarily to the fact that when in your mouth the wine is closer to your smelling region. As well, the wine warms up in the mouth, and the warmer the wine the more volatiles released, and the more volatiles released the more prominent the odor, and the more prominent the odor the easier it is to identify. By and large, a great deal of what is thought to be *taste* is really just **in-mouth** odors. Simply pinch your nose shut and see how little you really do taste without your nose or recall your last cold when your nasal passages were congested. It's almost as if your sense of taste disappeared.

Some wine and taste authorities prefer to describe that first method, inhaling, as smelling. Not much to argue about there. But to the second, exhaling odors from the mouth through the nose, they define as savoring. A few get quite insistent about differentiating between the two. At the risk of incurring their learned disapproval I choose to disagree with them. Smelling is smelling, whichever direction the airflow. To savor something suggests an *intensity* of examination, not a direction of airflow. I take this recalcitrant stance not out of personal bravado but because both Master Webster and Master Oxford seem to agree with my definition of savor, or should I say I agree with theirs. So as you happen upon the word **smell** in this book it defines odors from both inhaling and exhaling.

Now, how does this all relate to wine tasting?

The first step in your olfactory examination of a wine, after sticking your nose well into the glass, is to breathe deeply. Normal breathing *breathing* allows only 5-10% of the inhaled air to reach the upper nasal passages and subsequently your personal smelling instrument — not at all conducive to making accurate judgments. So, a couple of short, deep sniffs are necessary. Then sit back and mentally analyze the wine odors. But now, wait a minute or so before taking another sniff of the same wine.

Despite the awesome sensitivity of our nose it possesses another very unique characteristic. It can *adapt* to smells by ignoring them, blocking them out completely. And this is generally to our benefit. If this were not true and, for example, first thing in the morning you were to apply a prominent smelling perfume or cologne, one with good staying power, that's about all you would smell for the day. It would simply overpower most other smells by being so close to you.

However, the nose, once it has identified an odor, proceeds to push that one smell into the background, allowing you to smell the other odors you meet daily. So, if you were to continue immediately sniffing the same wine you would soon lose the ability to smell that wine at all. By spacing out your sniffs you avoid the nose's ability to adjust to that wine's aroma and bouquet. Many a novice taster has wondered why his initial impression of a wine seemed so much better than later assessments. Now you know one cause — smelling without long enough intervals between sniffs.

In a more general fashion this principle of *adaption* can also affect your overall sensory impression of a wine. As you continue drinking the same wine over a period of let's say an evening you may have noticed how the wine never quite lives up to your first impression. It does really, but you've begun to adapt to that wine, taking its qualities a little for granted. The moral of this story — test first, then drink. Don't try to evaluate wines after you've been drinking them for a period of time.

Some very experienced wine tasters suggest (with certainly a degree of merit) that the only way to really evaluate a wine is by drinking the better part of the bottle, over a matter of a few hours. Granted, you may indeed achieve a certain intimacy with a wine that way but the practicality of this suggestion leaves a little to be desired, should there be a number of wines to taste.

Wine odors originate primarily from the more volatile esters and aldehydes of wine. But it's not a single odor you experience. It's a composite of dozens of different odors. The real task of the wine judge is to separate some of these smells and assess them individually.

Despite the scientific advances in separating and identifying odor compounds with machines judging wine still remains more of an art than a science. No mechanical or electronic instrument has yet been devised that is as sensitive as your nose.

Thankfully our memory banks are very well attached to our sense of smell, too. It's not often that we will have smelled something and then fail to recognize it when it presents itself again. And that's one talent you will want to cultivate. A good **memory** for smells is invaluable. It helps you identify the basic character of the wine, to be recalled and compared with other wines you'll drink in the years to come. Some experienced tasters have such well tuned memories, in this respect, they are able to recall easily wines they tasted decades ago.

Without developing such a memory you lose much of your capacity to make quality comparisons. Most often it's by comparison to a known set of standards that you can evaluate the stature of a wine.

Not only should we recognize the importance of the nose in wine judging but we should also realize that the nose and our sense of smell represent a genuine gap in our sensory education.

Much time and effort is spent in training other inferior human senses. I'm thinking of the training we give our ear, for music and the spoken word. Our sense of sight is cultivated and taught to appreciate various forms of art, design and color combinations. But how many have ever attended a smelling class, in any institution of learning? It's all but an ignored discipline. Most take it for granted. "We can all smell, can't we?" Most of us, yes! But do we know fully what it is we're smelling and how to differentiate between one smell and another similar to it?

Think of the fragrant smell of freshly mown grass, leaves burning in the Fall, a chicken roasting in the oven, a baby fresh from a bath. They're unforgettable. As powerful and sensitive as the nose is, with a little exercise and concentration it can become a facet of your senses to be appreciated far more than it is now.

TOUCH

Having passed by the eyes and nose we've now reached the mouth and our consideration of your sense of **touch**. The primary instrument you'll employ is, of course, your tongue, since it's still considered a little crude and somewhat impractical to stick your fingers in the glass to feel the texture of the wine that way.

Two basic factors about wine are identified and evaluated by your sense of touch, the **body** or texture and the **astringency** (tannin content) of the wine. For most, the most sensitive area of touch in the mouth is down the centre of the tongue. The insides of our cheeks, the roof of our mouth, the lips and so on are capable of **tactile** (touch)

The Tongue
A Sensory Tool

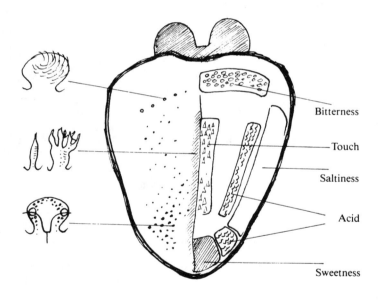

The tongue has a sensory geography. If put to proper use it can become far more valuable to the winetaster than is normally expected.

sensations but are in need of the tongue to accurately accomplish the more delicate evaluations.

We also run into what are technically termed *kinesthetic* (mechanical) impressions that are related to touch. Some common examples are the prickly sensation from both natural and artificial carbonation and a burning or hot feeling from the alcohol content. Even highly acidic wines, like Portugal's Vinhos Verdes, can stimulate our tactile sensors in this mechanical manner.

A very common wine additive, sulphur, if present in large enough quantities may become evident in a physical way as well as in its odor form. It does so by causing those individuals sensitive enough to sneeze. Technically, it's the trigeminal nerve endings in the mouth and nose that react in such an abrupt manner. This is not a frequent event but common enough to bring it to your attention.

A more elaborate consideration of how you determine the body of a wine is found in chapter 4 under the **Tactile** heading. Astringency, the other tactile sensation, is important as one means of estimating the potential life span of a wine. Further details can be found under that same heading in chapter 4.

TASTE

You've got about three thousand of them in four varieties. No, you can't be taxed for them (not yet anyway). They're just little bumps on your tongue called *papillae* (taste buds) and each one is connected to the brain by a nerve. Without them you would be minus your ability to *taste*, in the true sense of the word.

Of all our senses one of the poorest, one of the least exacting is **taste**. In fact it's downright primal, in comparison to our sense of smell. For all intents and purposes our taste sensitivity depends solely on those three thousand taste buds on your tongue. It sounds like 3,000 would be more than enough to do an admirable job. But with all those taste buds you sense only four very basic stimulations — **saltiness, sweetness, acidity** (sourness), and **bitterness**. And for our immediate purposes we can ignore saltiness, as wine contains little salt, certainly not usually at levels you can sense, unless you count those *cooking* wines that have salt added to them to circumvent those

Most people are shy to use it – but do – the bucket is a legitimate tasting device.

governments who monopolize sale of alcoholic beverages. By having a certain salt content they are no longer considered legally to be wines and subsequently you do find them on the shelves of the local grocery store. Some wines that have been subjected to 'ion-exchange resins', used to prevent tartrate precipitation, will occasionally demonstrate a "saltiness" that is perceptible to some tasters. This is usually the result of a poor application of this procedure.

Our taste sensitivity can be affected by both psychological and physiological influences. So allowances must be made for your frame of mind and physical well being at the time of tasting. And it seems our taste, most of our sensory devices, are really keenest when the individual is hungry. I don't think this is just cause to starve your wine-tasting guests, but do your tasting first followed by whatever edibles you have in mind.

Thankfully the nose and tongue work well in tandem. Often taste alone is just not enough, as a number of substances stimulate the taste buds in exactly the same way. Without the nose's ability to further evaluate the odor we would be unable to distinguish between the tastes.

However, we don't want to appear as if we're putting the sense of taste down too much. After all, it is still a vital **key** that needs to be consulted before any final conclusions about a wine can be reached.

The tongue has its own sensory geography, too. The most effective **sour** (acid) sensors are located on the upper edges of the tongue; **bitterness** is sensed more accurately by taste buds on the rear surface of the tongue, while **sweetness** sensors found on the tip of the tongue work best. For interest sake, saltiness is detected on the sides of your *clapper*.

These various locations partially explain why you see wine judges and those so-called *connoisseurs* doing all that sloshing and gurgling during a tasting. Some colorfully term this *chewing* the wine, but I like sloshing and gurgling better. Besides, the only things I can chew are things I can bite. And any wine you can bite has a shade too much body for me.

It's common for most wine experts during a tasting to spit (expell) most of the wine into a bucket or some such receptacle after tasting it. This action is not a demonstration of how they felt about the quality of the wine. There's good reason for it. After tasting and swallowing a few dozen wine samples you can appreciate how a taster's accuracy would soon decline in direct proportion to the number of samples. So, for self-preservation, a bucket please!

But should you spit it all out, without swallowing any? Some professionals insist, and rightly so, at least a small amount of the wine should be swallowed to bring into play the *pharynx* (the muscular tube connecting the mouth cavity to the esophagus). Here, taste and tactile sensations seem to linger awhile (aftertaste) allowing you to better assess the overall *flavor* and *finish* (the lasting impression) of the wine.

SUMMARY

My selection of these points and their order of presentation has not been arbitrary. We've been following the very natural sequence of our own senses. In fact, each time you partake of a glass of wine you follow this sequence without even having to think about it.

When a wine is presented to you your first impression is what you see, it's **visual**. Unless you're blindfolded or in a very dark room you can't help but see the wine first.

Following this, even if you were to immediately bring the glass to your mouth to take a sip it's difficult to avoid **smelling** it before that first drop touches your lips. So whether it was your intention or not, you've remained true to the pattern so far . . . visual to olfactory (nose).

Once that first drop does reach your mouth, again, though your intention may have been to simply drink it, your sense of **touch** comes automatically into play as first, physical contact is made with the wine. Only then does it finally reach your tastebuds and a final **taste** impression registers.

Unconsciously you have been following the very pattern professional wine tasters pursue — Visual — Olfactory (nose) — Tactile (touch) — Taste. It's the natural way.

Now that some of the factors that can influence the use of your sensory tools have been detailed the time has arrived to put them to work. Just how it is you're going to use these tools is the subject of the next few chapters. Use them wisely and accurately and they will reward you with an insight into wine that will significantly increase both your knowledge and enjoyment.

The Natural Tasting Sequence

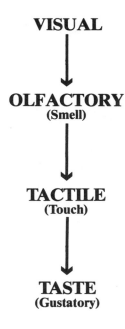

VISUAL

OLFACTORY
(Smell)

TACTILE
(Touch)

TASTE
(Gustatory)

Visual – the first clue to the quality of all wines. Be careful not to be misled, though.

A Sight To See 2

VISUAL

As already mentioned, it's quite difficult to avoid making visual judgments about wine first. We see a glass of this glorious nectar and immediately our sense of sight has made an assessment, of sorts.

The task at hand though, is to focus that ability and evaluate two specific visual aspects of wine — its general **appearance** and its **color**. This may at first sound preposterously simple, but there is truly more than meets the eye, if you'll pardon the pun.

Since these two aspects should be considered separately we'll start with . . .

Appearance

Our prime concern under the heading of Appearance is for the *clarity* of the wine, as well as for the condition of the surface (meniscus) or *disc* of the wine. A limpid, crystalline appearance can be the very first indication of a truly **great** or **fine** wine. An **ordinary**, a severely blended, or a straight out **poor** wine will frequently demonstrate a dull, lack-lustre appearance. But a note of caution.

Modern wine production methods must be given special consideration here. With the advent of new filtering and polishing processes wines of very insignificant stature can be produced easily and economically, with a very fine, enhanced appearance. Of course, that may be their sole redeeming merit, but they still look great and we must be aware of the possible reasons for this good first impression.

To describe wine **clarity** we use such words as *brilliant* for a perfect crystal-clear appearance, *bright* for something slightly less, and *clear* for an acceptable clarity. On the negative side, *dull* would indicate a minor fault, *hazy* a serious problem, and *cloudy* could be totally unacceptable. Be careful here, when you're judging wines that may have been chilled, whites more probably. A very fine *mist* can coat the glass (condensation) and create a cloudy impression.

Start your visual examination by first considering the upper surface (meniscus) of the wine. First, view it almost at eye level and then look straight down on it. It should be bright, shiny and reflective.

If not, if it's flat or dull assess it as a negative factor. At best, it will indicate simply an ordinary wine, at worst, some potentially serious faults with that bottle.

Occasionally you will stumble across a wine with an irridescence, a film of sorts, floating on its surface. This may be indicative of a number of very grave wine ailments such as the growth of microorganisms or enzymatic problems. Such factors could lead to the wine being oxidized if its source is yeast or to vinegariness if the problem stems from a bacteria.

Poor handling of the wine could also cause this surface irridescence, from machinery oil getting into the wine during processing or on rare occasions it could result from an excessive iron content. There are a number of other technical surface faults like *mycoderma vini* and *aceti*, which are whitish and greyish films but we'll stop at this point before this turns into a rather feeble attempt at being a scientific paper on the subject. Besides you probably know more about this factor than you want to by now.

That's also why we want to make it clear that your job is not necessarily to identify which of these faults prevails or its original cause. They will all be judged as negatives and will be recorded appropriately in your numerical evaluation.

Pressing on with our visual inspection, we can approach the actual aspect of wine **clarity**. Using a white background or a backlight of some sort you now look through the wine for suspended particles.

Decanting may become necessary when sediment is discovered.

Again a note of caution is sounded as not all factors which may cause a wine to be *temporarily* hazy or cloudy are negatives, ultimately.

With the growing consumer demand for what amounts to a clinical clarity for all wines, it's becoming increasingly difficult to convince some people of the validity of the previous statement. But there are legitimate reasons why a wine may *temporarily* display a haziness. Too often this sight alone puts off the inexperienced wine drinker who, without further investigation, proceeds to pass over such a wine, when it may indeed have been a genuine delight.

This temporary haziness, in fact, may be a fine, well-aged wine (more often a red) quite naturally *throwing a sediment*, as the expression is used in the wine world. In the early stages of leaving this natural deposit (primarily of color matter) the suspended particles can be quite noticeable. However, it clears as the sediment drops to the bottom of the bottle or clings tenaciously to the sides.

The degree of deposit will depend greatly on the depth of the wine's original color. As deposits continue the color alters, reds becoming more brown and whites taking on amber shades. **Fine** white wines that age well only throw a sediment after many years of proper ageing.

Once this process has fairly well run its course and the bottle has rested or remained in one position for a period of time (a few days preferably) the wine should be quite clear. But on serving or transporting the wine the sediment may become disturbed, thus you could be momentarily confronted with a hazy wine that was clear only moments ago.

An experienced wine judge will take all this into consideration, watching carefully for the handling of the wine and its age. So, a **fine**, aged wine roughly handled, with its natural sediment disturbed, despite its displaying a haziness, should not be prematurely judged as having a fault. *Decanting* may be necessary.

Decanting (removing the wine from the bottle to another container) can present you with some rather awkward moments, though. The sediment may cling tightly to the side of the bottle making it fairly easy to decant. However, the deposits can also be very light and easily disturbed. Often your only option is to pour it through some fine gauze, and then very carefully. But with wines of this nature it will be well worth the extra care and attention.

This whole matter indicates the value of one major principle you would do well to keep in mind for all your wine judging. The more you know about the wine the more accurate will be your evaluations. *Blind tastings* can be a challenge, a test of your growing wine sensitivity. But remember, *evaluating* a wine is not a contest. It's a genuine attempt to establish the quality of that individual bottle of wine. It's purpose — to help you purchase wisely while learning from the experience.

It was a pleasure to read similar comments, so well expressed, in two other wine books. Alexis Bespalof in his **"Wine – A Complete Introduction"** released in 1980, conveyed the thought succinctly. He said:

*"It's often assumed, by the way, that wine experts are people who can taste wines whose labels have been covered up and then name the vineyard and vintage. Although some members of the wine trade amuse themselves by putting their colleagues through such blind tastings, the real skill of a wine buyer is demonstrated in exactly the **opposite** manner. He stands in a particular cellar, tasting a specific wine, and has even noted the barrel from which it was drawn. He must now determine how good it is, how good it will be six months or six years later, and what it is worth. It is precisely this ability to concentrate on the wine at hand – in order to **judge its value**, not guess its origin – that is the primary attribute of his expertise."*

And in the Signet Book of **"American Wine"** third edition, Peter Quimme (the team) asserted boldly, *"Assessing wines blind is common in wine tasting; identifying them blind is a stunt. To **identify** wines is not the point of tasting, appreciation or even connoisseurship. The point is **evaluation**."*

Amen!

This all may sound quite reasonable in this context but you may or may not appreciate that these comments and views, in a number of wine circles, verge on sheer heresy.

For many decades now the objective of a good number of influential wine *afficionados* has been to develop the ability to identify a wine's place of origin. And this was supposed to be a comment on quality. If it ever was, it certainly is no longer true today.

Many of those *classic* wine regions have, shall we say, altered over the years, with many new wine regions in various corners of the globe challenging the traditional classics with wines that occasionally surpass them. After all, identifying *which* wine it is says little about *how good* it is. Most often the very factors that distinguish one wine from another, as a personality let's say, are non-qualitative factors to begin with.

At the risk of sounding repetitious — the objective of wine tasting is to **evaluate quality**. Only then can you judge whether or not your wine money has been well spent.

But now, back to the point of wine *clarity* . . . before we create the erroneous impression that haziness or cloudiness is only rarely a negative factor let's look at the darker side of the picture for a few moments. *Haziness* or worse, *cloudiness* is most often the warning sign of a very serious problem with wine. It could warn of an undesirable yeast growth or what is called a protein imbalance. An excess of iron can also cause a milkiness. If the cloudiness is accompanied by a crystalline deposit, a harmful excess of potassium bitartrate (tartaric acid) or calcium tartrate may exist.

We should not forget this one point, however. Tartrate crystals in a clear wine are nothing to be concerned with. They may appear as tiny flakes or crystals at the bottom of the bottle or be adhering to the bottom of the cork. They offer no impairment to the wine and should not reflect negatively in your scoring. White wines seem to be most affected this way. But, accompanied by a *cloudiness*, and we do have a genuine fault on our hands. See page 43.

Flocculation is another fault you may run into. It's a very technical term used to describe a cluster of *tuft-like* particles, usually caused by an undesirable yeast growth. But again, your function is not to play scientific detective and sort out the various causes of these faults but simply rate their positive and negative affects on the wine. Although this is probably more technical than the average winedrinker will want to pursue this matter there is a practical side to all this. Knowing which is a genuine fault and which isn't will save many a bottle from the sad destiny of being poured down the kitchen sink, unnecessarily.

Because of those earlier discussed technical advances in the filtration and polishing of liquids, **poor** and **great** wines too often seem to stand as equals, in this one respect. Wine *clarity* as a measure of wine quality has declined somewhat in its significance over the years, especially in the last two decades. Yet, we can't simply ignore it. It remains one of the keys in assessing wine quality and potential problems in the wine. Perhaps then, its weight, its overall significance to the wine judging process, should be adjusted downwards, remaining a factor to be noted, but with less importance than it once held.

Color

There's one fact we must come to grips with first, in any consideration of wine **color**. It would take an encyclopedia to list all the possible color variations. And no printer would be capable of reproducing all the exact shades and their various nuances. So, from the outset we must realize our limitations.

Each wine has its individual color and scope, or range of colors, it will span during its lifetime. For the most part age is the factor which causes the wine to travel its full color range . . . at varying rates, quite naturally. Grape variety, soil conditions, weather, cellar practices and a number of additional elements combine to produce wine colors that are unique to that particular wine. Only experience will teach you to recognize and remember the subtle differences.

It wasn't my intention to start us off on a negative foot with this point. For, indeed there is a great deal we can learn from that broad range or spectrum of wine colors, those we can easily recognize. Evaluation of these broader color groupings can go a long way to help us determine the quality and maturity of each wine that crosses our path.

Before discussing these general color categories and what they mean, several cautionary notes are needed.

Appreciation of any color is a very subjective and individual matter. This very fact alerts us to be wary of being influenced by personal color preferences. Unless you're careful your personal color likes and dislikes could very well *color* your judgment. The remedy . . . (a) keep foremost in mind the color standards we're going to discuss and what they indicate for wine quality, (b) ignore your pet shades.

Just to add to your considerations, you should be aware that the winemaker can do much to, shall we say, supplement a wine that has poor color. By simply blending his wine with wine made from certain other grapes he can significantly improve the look of his own product. Those certain grapes (teinturiers) are varieties whose singular merit may be their deep, dark color. This blending will most often improve only the visual aspect of the wine, not its many other necessary qualities. But a wine judge must be aware of this possibility and once he has considered the other aspects of the wine and discovers that the **visual** factors are grossly exaggerated by comparison he then will understand what may have taken place. It simply reaffirms the old adage "looks can be deceiving."

As well, keep in mind our earlier consideration of the influences both lighting and background can have on your color judgments. This is especially important since you're utilizing the weakest of your senses, your eyes. So do take some care in choosing your setting.

But just what are we looking for as far as color is concerned?

Two major factors! **Tint** or hue and the **depth** or density of the color (some authorities refer to this as luminance). Let's deal with the latter attribute first, **depth** of color.

Two wines may have a tint or hue quite similar but vary considerably in their *depth* of color. A very simple experiment can be done with a red wine. Using too identical wine glasses, half fill one glass with the selected wine. Before doing the same for the second glass dilute some of the wine in another glass at about a 3 wine to 1 water ratio. Now half fill the second glass with the diluted wine. The volume of fluid is obviously the same. Now, look down from the top of the glass, through the wine. Make sure you use a white background. You'll immediately notice the pure wine has a deeper color. It is actually more opaque, more difficult to see through.

Another illustration . . . lightly stroking a piece of paper with a crayon, then pressing down hard, several times, over the same spot produces marks of the same color but one mark has obviously much more density to it. It's darker. It is also physically more dense, with more crayon material on the paper, causing the added color. Our sample wines are not different in this respect. The darker shade of the pure wine is caused by literally more color *pigments* in that volume of liquid. This same principle applies to wines in their natural state.

The color pigments found in each grape variety (in the skin) also demonstrate different degrees of resistance to extraction. Most of these pigments are not generally all that soluable in water. They are in alcohol, however. So if the wine is allowed to ferment on the skins the alcohol extracts the pigments to greater depths of color, varying

Harmless Tartrate Crystals are often called "Wine Diamonds".

according to the grape variety.*

What do these various color depths indicate?

Several possibilities, in general terms. In a positive vein, good color depth may denote good tannin content from fully ripened grapes, thusly a wine that should age well, benefiting from its years. Also, it may mean that the wine has been allowed a reasonable length of time in contact with its skins, giving it added fruit, bouquet, as well as those added years.

White wines are becoming almost an exception to this as more and more producers are fermenting the white juice minus the skins . . . the skins having been removed beforehand.

Depending on what the rest of your evaluations reveal good color density could also signify grapes grown in a very sunny climate. Usually these grapes with heavy, sun-thickened skins produce wines of very **ordinary** overall stature but will possess great depth of color. These grapes (teinturiers) are frequently those types we spoke of earlier, used for blending with other wines of weaker coloring.

A pale color, though often simply a characteristic of certain grape varieties, could also indicate a fast, poor vinification process. Or, it could indicate too high a yield per acre causing low extract in the harvested grapes. An inferior vintage originating from too few sun

---

Winemakers these days have alternative methods of extracting color pigments from the skins, (e.g. using heat) then adding it back to the wine, having fermented the juice separate from the skins.

hours during the growing season will also fail to produce the required pigments in the grape skin and as expected a weak, low density color results.

There are more factors we could identify but again, we must keep in mind our task is not so much to identify the precise reason for the deficiency but to determine its degree and evaluate it accordingly.

Window dressing is a phrase used by some wine authorities to designate a wine that has excellent visual qualities, both appearance and color, but fails to follow through in most other respects. We must be cautious we are not led too far astray by a wine's glorious *robe*, as wine colors are called in France.

While sound color is definitely an ingredient contributing to the overall quality of a wine there are numerous wines which have poor *depth* of color yet are quite acceptable or may even excell in all other aspects. Be careful not to quickly create in your mind a negative feeling for such a wine for this singular deficiency.

Now, to that other color key **hue** or tint, the actual *color* differences themselves and what they mean.

Each wine has its own color and each color its own tale to tell. The limitless variations in **hue** originate from a number of sources. Grape variety, maturity, time on the vine, length of fermentation on the skins, climate conditions for that particular vintage, soil make-up, general cellar practices, etc. are all elements which affect the final color (tint) of the wine. However, these limitless variations can be grouped into several broad color ranges which can reveal a number of facets of that wine.

RED WINE

Red, as a wine color, originates from the pigments in the grape skin (anthocyanol pigments) which are extracted primarily during fermentation. And it's to be expected that should the wine be of sufficient quality to age beneficially that many of these color pigments will in time precipitate out of the liquid and create a sediment. This *dropping out* of the color matter is one direct cause for the shift in color from a youthful purple to the nearly brown shade in a wine of venerable years.

Now, to some specifics!

Purple is indeed, generally the color of youth and immaturity. It implies a wine freshly fermented, a wine still wearing diapers, so to speak. Most red wines, as a type of wine, will at least start their life with something of this shade, progressing towards other fascinating hues as it matures. The precise time needed to make these vital transformations from youth, to adolescence, to maturity is governed by grape variety, depth of original color and a number of handling practices in the winery. Yet, like some people, who never grow up, a few, usually poorer quality wines, may never leave this infantile purple stage. They may have neither the breed nor the time, as they will be consumed, some before they ever reach the bottle, others long before their second birthday.

In addition to these wines that are consumed so young there are a number of native North American varieties and hybrids that have such strong pigments in this color range that their purple blush never really disappears all together. It remains an identifiable characteristic throughout their various stages of ageing.

Ruby is the next step. Assuming that the wine is a **fine** wine or certainly a better **vin ordinaire**, it will continue to make progress, at least to this point. This is the shade immediately following the loss of that newly vinted purple tone. Perhaps the wine has reached two or more years of age, having finished any wood ageing* and is now resting quietly in bottle.

For those better **vin ordinaires** that fall into this category they may well be on the retailers' shelves, having reached their personal pinnacle. Many have been produced with this lifespan in mind and are often referred to as *commercial grade* wines. For some of the truly **fine** wines a further stage or two may lie ahead.

Red, true red, the color of adolescence for wine, marks the traditional period between youth and full maturity. Some wines, however, will demonstrate shades more like *garnet* at this stage. The best of the vin ordinaires and some of the more humble fine wines should be drunk at this stage as further ageing will do them little good (2-4 years of age).

---

*Some time variations in the color progression can be influenced by such factors as wood ageing as opposed to bottle ageing . . . the wine ageing more slowly in bottle. Also, good screw-on caps can retard the ageing process when compared to corks.

Red/Brown or brick-red is definitely a sign of maturity in well-handled wines. The brownish tinge is first noticed at the edge, where the wine touches the glass. I use the term well-handled because this shade can also result from too much exposure to air (oxidation). A quick sniff, however, should tell you immediately whether the wine is *oxidized* or not. (see Glossary for description)

There are also those rather impatient producers who will try to circumvent the time needed to reach these advanced stages by employing some short-cuts. Usually they heat the wines for a period of time trying to create a semblance of age. But such wines will frequently exhibit a cooked, madeirized (Madeira-like) taste easily identifiable and really not worth the effort in the end. Many truly **fine** wines will reach their peak at this stage, further ageing doing them few favors (5-10 years).

Mahogany represents a shade few wines ever achieve . . . in good shape. This is primarily true because few have the inherent stamina to attain this plateau and still be worth drinking. By far the vast majority of all wine (80% or more) are **poor** to **ordinary** at best and once to the red stage decline quickly into senility. Some extremely **fine** and truly **great** wines of noble character and classic variety will reach the softer, more subtle red/brown tint of mahogany, with strength to spare. It most often represents ten to fifteen years, or more, in bottle and such vigorous wines may remain essentially in this superior condition for another ten, twenty, or more years before a serious decline in quality becomes evident.

But keep in mind we're talking about the elite of the wine world. Less, far less than five percent of any vintage will ever aspire to such lofty heights. And in some years no vineyard will sire a wine that attains this plateau of excellence.

Amber/Brown shades cause polite professional disagreement among wine authorities. For some tasters, this means three strikes and out. The wine is over the hill in their view, hardly worth drinking. There's no doubt it represents a wine of advanced age but for other experts this senectuous robe and its associated qualities are still to be admired and savored.

I'm not about to even attempt to help you resolve this point, either.

You'll just have to experience this stage for yourself and formulate your own conclusions.

Inferior wines may, however, acquire a similar appearance within a very few years. But, smelling and tasting them should quickly inform you that their funeral took place, or should have, quite some time ago.

WHITE WINE

You have a slight advantage judging white wines. The human eye is more capable of sensing **tint** differences in the yellow/green region of the color spectrum.

Of course, when we speak of *white* wines we do so euphemistically, as no wine, or grape for that matter, is truly white in color. We're actually talking about a range of colors from a *watery yellow/green* to a *rich gold/brown*. Sweet white table wines, generally speaking, display deeper shades of yellow right from the beginning. With bottle age *gold* hues begin to appear then turn to definite light brownish tinges in advanced age.

Frequently in wine writing you will come across the word *straw* to denote a certain white wine tint. But this has always confused me. Having spent some time "on the land" I've seen straw with a definite greenish tinge, to that which was a bright yellow/gold. For me the term *straw* does not consistently bring to mind one particular shade. If those who are used to using this descriptive term will forgive me, I'll avoid using this word during our discussions.

Pale Yellow/Green, this is a shade particularly common to wines grown in cooler climates, where the grapes may not have ripened fully. The greenish tinge will be especially noticeable in young, dry wines (residual chlorophyll). Chardonnay and Riesling grape varieties will occasionally demonstrate this quality. White wines from the warmer climates rarely exhibit these greenish tinges.

A few years in bottle, however, should transform any touches of green to pale yellows. If not, it may arouse some legitimate suspicions that excess amounts of sulphur added to the wine are retarding the normal ageing process thus the natural color progression. One purpose of adding sulphur in the first place is to inhibit the *browning* of the fruit. But some producers go a little overboard, trying to keep their wines young-looking forever.

Light Yellow, is the most common *hue* for young, dry white table wines. This is not suggesting that there won't be numerous variations and depths of color within this chromatic range. Only experience can teach you the minute differences. For most wines in this category this will be their ultimate color achievement and they should be joyfully consumed at this point (1-3 years of age).

Yellow/Gold, shades are most frequently associated with sweeter table wines, primarily during their youth. Wines like Sauternes, the Beerenausleses from Germany, genuine Tokays from Hungary, and the Vins Jaunes of France. A few drier white table wines will attain colors similar to this after 3 to 4 years of bottle age, especially if they've received some wood ageing.

Gold, this is the next stage of color development for these luscious sweet dessert wines as they quietly slumber decades or more in bottle. Some **fine** and **great** dry table wines will also approximate this shade after 5 to 6 years, with perhaps less depth of color.

Yellow/Brown, for many authorities, signifies absolutely too much ageing for any dry table wine. Or, it could also be the tell-tale sign of early oxidation, that arch-enemy of wine. Bad storage and too much light can also be the villain. For those heavier, sweet varieties it could mark 20 to 100 years after their vintage and for them much remains to be appreciated by the most discriminating connoisseur.

ROSÉ WINE

Like both red and white, **rosé** as a color does not confine itself to describing a singular shade. Rosé wines vary widely in *tint* and *depth* of coloring, according to the very different styles produced in various wine districts of the world. The better rosés are vinted from quality black grapes, the skins remaining in contact with the crushed juice just long enough (5-48 hours) to tint the wine to the desirable degree. Inferior rosés are occasionally due to blending red and white grapes. But rarely do you find rosés that are simply a blend of red and white wines. This is the case not only because of the poor quality wine that results but it is illegal in some lands.

To acquire a good, firm color for rosé it takes some very careful handling and judgment on the part of the winemaker. So it is not always the compromise wine some believe it to be nor is it simply a second class red wine, as some also view it.

Since most rosés respond rather poorly to the march of time and most, if not all of their charm is in their vernal freshness, age is unquestionably their foe. They are usually bottled quite quickly (early in the following Spring) with little or no contact with wood (ageing in barrel).

To wait longer than two years before drinking most rosés would be, with the rarest exception (eg. some rosés from Tavel in France), too long. Chances are you will have missed their prime by a year or more.

Rosé, the standard rosé tint is not just a weak, low density red but a solid Rosé color.

It should be a clear firm shade. This is one indication of a quality rosé. Only the slightest tinge of orange or purple is forgivable, but it will still be a compromise from the standard.

Pink/Orange is a common shade for several types of rosés made from grape varieties like the Grenache. Especially is this the case if the fruit is grown in warmer climates. While producing pleasant wines this shade is not indicative of the better quality rosés.

Pink suggests a note of artificiality from too much winery involvement. A vivid *pink* color with blue or purple tinges may even indicate an unhealthy state, either high pH (low acid) or poor fining (a filtering stage). Metal contamination can also cause a bold pink tint.

Salmon/Pink is another inferior shade. It may be caused by the grape being picked too late or our old spoiler oxidation has been at work again. Any hint of this brownish tint is definitely a negative factor and should be evaluated as such.

SUMMARY

It should be apparent at this point, there are some severe limitations in our ability to assess, with total accuracy, the Visual aspects of wine. Again, this is true because we are employing the weakest of the four senses, our eyes, while trying to put into words the impossible, all the nuances and shadings of wine colors.

This helps us to appreciate the need for a total sensory evaluation of each wine. Exploring one or two facets is not enough. A complete, composite, sensory profile must be made for each wine before you render a final judgment. But this does not have to be a long, complicated and formal analysis. With a little practice you can use this method of wine analysis, step-by-step, in a very casual manner, while you're drinking any wine. For the more formal evaluations you can bring out the rating sheets and all the other paraphernalia you need to make an in depth investigation.

Yet, on the positive side of the **Visual** coin, what we have been able to consider will most certainly go a long way to assist you in evaluating the general quality of the majority of table wines you'll come across, by both their **color** and **appearance**. In the final analysis you've made a few, significant steps forward and unlocked a few doors in your appreciation of this entire subject of wine evaluation, with several more to come.

Candling the wine in a Burgundy Cellar.

Nosing Around 3

OLFACTORY

At last we've reached your most precise wine sense, your nose. Assuming that it's in fairly decent working order, minus any major obstructions, we can proceed with some of the most significant quality assessments you'll make in this whole evaluation procedure. And when you do get to the more serious occasions for tasting wine try to avoid the situations that can hinder your nose from doing its phenomenal job. Smoke in the room, strong deodorants, perfumes, colognes, flowers, food smells, etc. can only make your delightful task more difficult, certainly less pleasant (see page 85 for additional details).

Your nose is used to explore three major facets . . . the **intensity** of wine odors, the **aroma**, and the **bouquet**. One of its major challenges will be to both discover and evaluate the positive elements and also to ferret out faults that will detract from the stature of the wine.

Wine odors originate from three major sources . . . from the **fruit**, the grape itself, from the **vinification** process, and from **ageing** the wine. The grapes, of course, possess their own unique identity and pass this on, in varying degrees, to the wine. Vinification creates new

Swirling the wine allows more volatiles to be released making your "nosing" job much easier.

odor compounds, bi-products of the fermentation and processing. With time will come additional fragrances that originate from wood and bottle ageing. To give yourself the best opportunity to sense these odors a glass that holds at least 6-10 oz. should be used . . . one that is narrower at the opening than the body. This traps and funnels or channels the odors to your nose.

Swirl the wine first. By swirling the wine in your glass you increase the surface area of the wine while agitating and aerating it. This action aids in releasing more of the *volatiles*, making your smelling job a little easier. It may take some practice to achieve a smooth swirling motion, sans the spills that can occur. So, for beginners, make sure there's nothing close at hand you don't want covered in wine. Try it first with the glass resting on the table. (See page 52.)

But first to the *strength* of all these odors, the . . .

Intensity

When it comes to wine smells there are a number of special synonyms for intensity, words like *strength, prominence, force,* and if you want to be a trifle more colorful, terms such as *muscle* and *punch* will suffice. A bit cavalier perhaps, but nevertheless they do help us to appreciate this particular quality. **Intensity** can range from being virtually *non-existent,* to *light,* to *full,* to *very intense.*

Wines soundly vinted from grapes of the more noble varieties often possess a more distinctive character. In one manner, this is detected by the *intensity* of their odors. The smell of very **fine** or **great** wine seems to linger in the glass long after the last desirable drop has stimulated the palate of some appreciative wine lover. Poorer quality grapes (for winemaking purposes) tend to have a very *light* odorous intensity (poor character) or, they can be overly intense (eg. some native North American and Muscat varieties). They're persistent, their aroma never seems to go away no matter how intensely you wish it would.

Often, vineyards that produce high yields per acre (too many tons of grapes due to too little pruning) produce grapes of lower quality and character. They exhibit weaker color and flavor extracts so it's little wonder they have diminished intensity.

Before you evaluate the intensity factor and rate it accordingly you must sort out one additional complication. You must ask yourself, is what I'm smelling the maximum intensity of a fully developed wine, in

53

other words the best it's ever going to get? Or, am I experiencing the same level of intensity from a wine that has yet to reach full maturity, the intensity of its nose increasing with time?

A little complicated, yes, but your visual inspection will have already helped you to determine the wine's approximate age. Judging, then that the wine is not fully developed and has more to come or, that's it, as far as this wine is concerned, will assist your appreciation of this factor.

If you are going to score this wine, using some evaluation system, you must assess it for what it is at this moment but you would certainly want to note whether you expect it to improve with age. Trying to *guess* at how this and other factors *might* improve with the passage of time is fine, even necessary. But these judgments should not be reflected in your rating at this time. As this and other factors improve they should receive an improved score, for if the wine is going to get better there must be room for the score to improve. So, while you may feel quite strongly that a certain element will improve . . . wait for it to do so before you give it the extra points.

There has been considerable debate and controversy over this very point for decades. And there are many notable winetasters who still feel you must reflect the wine's potential in your current scoring. If this reasoning be sound and you rate the wine as being truly **great** because it *may* achieve that status sometime in the future do you extend it the same scoring consideration when it is on the decline, (showing the negative signs of age), because at one point it *was* a **great** wine?

Again, it is not the goal of this book to attempt to resolve these thorny controversies but when the occasion demands, it must detail some of the processes that lead to the conclusions and views stated in these pages.

Although there are numerous potential faults in the nose of the wine, these are dealt with specifically under the heading **Bouquet.** Our concern at this point pertains solely to the strength or prominence of the wine's nose. This does not mean if it has a fault that produces a strong odor you would therefore score it well. The intensity of the nose must be clean, vinuous, without a major fault in either its bouquet or aroma, which brings us to that very topic . . .

Aroma

This term describes the group of wine odors that originate exclusively with the fruit, the fresh mature grapes. This helps us appreciate why the term is so often associated with the expression *fruitiness*. A wine described as being *fruity* will possess an **aroma** strongly characteristic of its grape variety. Italian wine-makers call it *fruttato*.

The aroma is more pronounced and distinctive during a wine's youth. As the wine matures the aroma declines in prominence to become a single element in the developing bouquet of the wine. With quality wines of considerable age the aroma may practically disappear, leaving only the complex odor of a mature bouquet. For 'vin ordinaires' the only remaining smell may simply be *vinuous* (see Glossary).

Technically, the aroma is created by the vaporization of certain elements found in the grapeskins. Fermentation plays a role in extracting these ingredients and this partially explains why for some grapes their chracteristic aroma is more pronounced *after* fermentation than it is from just the fresh, mature grapes themselves. Especially is this true with classic grapes like Riesling, Chardonnay, Pinot Noir, Sauvignon Blanc, and Gamay.

When choosing words to accurately describe a distinctive wine aroma often drawing a relationship to the fragrance of another, more commonly known fruit or plant is useful. It smells like fresh raspberries or violets, for example. You'll hear such expressions frequently in wine tasting circles. This is all well and good as long as you keep it under control. At times these associations can evade the most experienced taster's repertoire. Some individuals begin to compare wine aromas to fruits and flowers so exotic you need to compare them to other fruits and flowers for clarification. A friend once described the aroma of one wine as reminding him of the roses from his grandmother's garden, not just any roses mind you, but grandma's roses. Other than grandma few people will ever have much of an idea what he was talking about . . . the proverbial "failure to communicate". So, do be judicious; you could easily end up on a horticultural tangent moving away from the subject at hand, wine.

Keep in mind many grape varieties possess identifiable and distinctive aromas of their own and should be described in terms of their own aromas, this being sufficient for growing numbers of wine lovers to fully understand what is being described. On the whole you are better off learning to identify these aromatic wine characteristics than you are searching for colorful synonyms.

Several transformations during the wine making process will also have considerable influence on the level of fruit aroma. When left to ferment for a time on the skins, resulting wines will have more identifiable aroma (more aromatic elements are extracted from the skins). Sugar can also play a role. Wines that have retained some natural grape sugar will usually exhibit a more prominent aroma than wines that are bone dry. This is well illustrated in wines such as Asti Spumante with its high levels of residual sugar, as well as many of the white wines which have undergone prolonged cold fermentation and have varying levels of residual sugar.

So, a major point to remember under this heading is the pronounced difference between *aroma* and *bouquet*. They should never be confused with each other.

But how do you define Bouquet?

Bouquet

Aside from it sounding a little more distinguished and chic as a word **bouquet** describes a more elaborate and sophisticated odor. Basically, it defines the smells developed during the vinification process and by the wood and bottle ageing it may subsequently receive. As the wine approaches its maturity its bouquet is also achieving its full potential.

In more technical terms, the bouquet develops from the slow oxidation of the wine's fruit acids, esters, alcohols, etc., in wood and bottle. It's a far more complex and evasive odor than aroma.

Factors which affect and vary the intensity and make-up of the bouquet are grape variety, soil, weather, and processing (storage, cooperage, temperature, etc.). Cooler climates often produce higher levels of acid in the grapes so, often result in wines that develop more prominent bouquets.

Some fortified wines (alcohol added) possess very distinctive bouquets, easily identifiable. Certain Sherries, for example, have a bouquet with a strong raisin-like odor. Baked wines like Madeira and some North American versions of sherry have a caramel odor (hydrox-ymethyfurfural) that is also easy to recognize once you have isolated it and cataloged it in your odor memory bank.

Many young table wines, red, white, and rosé will, for a short period of time (a few months no more), possess a yeasty-like odor as part of their fermentation bouquet. This would certainly help you identify the age of the wine but this characteristic soon disappears, or should.

Wood, whether it's used for ageing wine in large vats or smaller cooperage (wooden barrels), introduces its own quality and character to the wine. It is said to give *complexity* to a wine, as a number of constituents are actually extracted from the wood and become part of the wine in both bouquet and taste. Our wine loving friends from Germany call it *Holzgeschmack*. For red wines it is, in most instances, a plus factor but, if too prominent it can also be a fault.

By the very natural extension of this thought it's not too difficult to surmise that each barrel could easily add its own very individual degree of character to the wine it contains. And indeed, this is frequently the case. Slight differences do become evident between identical wines taken from two separate barrels, sitting side by side. You are not likely to experience this in the wines you purchase as most producers, once the barrel ageing for that wine is completed, proceed to blend together all the wine of that type and vintage into large receptacles just before bottling, giving it a collective, consistent character.

As some wine authorities express varying opinions about the degree of woodiness desirable in red wines they more sharply differ in their views about any wood character at all in white wines. Some state categorically, **no wood** for whites, others make allowance for significant levels of this quality. Personally, I feel a certain touch of wood enhances *some* of the drier, classic whites made from grapes like Chardonnay and Sauvignon Blanc. While with fruity, fresh wines which are best drunk in their youth, a woody character is more of a negative influence. I'm thinking about table wines made from the Riesling family, Chenin Blanc, Muscats and Colombards, grapes of that nature.

As well as searching for and noting positive qualities in the bouquet there are several prominent faults that are identifiable to the nose. If detectable they will certainly lower your rating on this point.

An excess of **free sulphur** is definitely a negative factor (burning match smell.) With time this odor should decline and hopefully fall below the threshold of your being able to sense it at all. However, you should be aware that individuals' sensitivity to sulphur varies tremendously. In an attempt to introduce a friend to a lovely California white varietal the only response I got was his claim of a strong sulphur smell. I couldn't smell it but I later learned he can smell sulphur as easily as a bloodhound could track a skunk. If you have this unusual sensitivity you may have difficulty finding wines without a detectable trace of sulphur.

Another major fault concerns high **acetic acid** levels (vinegariness). You will find it easier to detect when you've taken a little of the wine into your mouth but it can be detected in the nose. Above .01 percent (1 part per 10,000) or approximately .7 grams per litre its obnoxious character becomes detectable to most wine drinkers.

Oxidation is another fault you will encounter occasionally. It's caused by a number of factors, but its pungent, burnt or caramelized smell is difficult to forget once you've pinned it down. A few pages back we spoke about the ageing process being "the *slow* oxidation" of certain components in the wine. This is not the oxidation we are referring to here. Proper oxidation, which ages a wine beneficially, takes place by minute amounts of air contacting the wine through a proper, quality cork. As a fault, we are talking about too much air coming into contact too quickly with the wine either in the processing or in the poor storage of the wine.

A simple exercise to re-create this odor is to leave a glass of *ordinary* red wine uncovered for several days. Then smell and taste it. It may be an exaggerated example but effective enough that you'll remember this element for quite some time.

If either **hydrogen sulfide** (a rotten egg smell) or **lactic acid** (a sauerkraut odor) are present at sufficient levels to be detected they too will be definite negatives on your nose checklist.

A *garlic,* oniony or *skunky* smell can indicate the off odor of **Mercaptans** (methyl and ethyl sulphides), originating from the chemical breakdown of the sulphur in some older wines or bacterial action in the presence of too much sorbic acid, a preservative used by some winemakers. Two other faulty odors frequently rearing their ugly noses, are a **moldy** and **corky** smell (like wet wood). Chemicals used in bleaching the corks can also create this odor.

Again, the corky smell is easier to detect once you've gotten a bit of the wine in your mouth. A frequent source of corkiness is a *diseased* cork. Occasionally, a bacteria (of the penicillum type) will even pass through the cork sterilization process and end up in your bottle of wine. Within a year or two it can start to affect the wine and once you've experienced a genuinely *corky* wine there will be little need for anyone to elaborate on the rotten wood smell the infected wine picks up.

There are other faults that do become detectable as part of a wine's nose but to be able to sense and competently identify them would take much concerted effort and practice, certainly more than an amateur interest in this whole subject. For the average wine lover the foregoing faults should be sufficient for you to separate the *good,* the *bad*, and the *undrinkable.*

SUMMARY

Your nose, that protuberance on the front of your face, is a key instrument for judging wine, no doubt. But, like any other faculty it needs exercise, in a disciplined manner. Its talents are many and its sensitivity awesome but it must be trained to focus on specifics.

There is no substitute for practical wine experience. Your written reactions to each of these experiences, filed away for future reference, will also help you grow and benefit from your wine judging abilities.

The task of distinguishing between *Aroma* and *Bouquet* is not a simple one. In fact, it may elude you for quite some time. But gradually, with time and practice, mixed liberally with a little persistence, each occasion you pour a glass of wine the differences will become more pronounced.

Sniff on!

Robert and Michael Mondavi (right) enjoy few things more than tasting their own renowned California products. A routine of daily tastings keeps them abreast of how each of their wines progress with age.

A Touching Chapter 4

Chapter

There comes the time when all this looking and smelling is simply not enough. Eventually you must put the wine into your mouth to feel, taste, and savor the rewards it has to offer.

But what do you do with it when it gets in there?

Does it lie there like a stagnant pool of rain water? Or is there really anything to all this sloshing and gurgling carried on by wine tasters, supposedly in the know?

There's no question, some of the oral antics of wine tasters, at times, appear to be rather, quaint, to put it politely. The noise alone can call their social graces into serious question. But all has a legitimate purpose.

The oral contortions, so clearly visible with experienced wine tasters, usually coincides with their attempts to move the wine to various areas of the tongue and inner mouth. The reason, as you will discover in the following few pages, is to concentrate the wine on various groups of taste buds, as some are more sensitive to certain components than others.

The gurgling results when the taster draws in air to mix with the wine. He does so to vaporize more of the wine, which in turn makes it easier to sense the various characteristics and components. There is definitely a knack to doing this without choking yourself or

Noble rot – Botrytis Cinerea (Latin) – Pourriture Noble (French) – Edelfaule (German) – Muffa Nobile (Italian) – whatever the language, it describes a beneficial mold that, under the proper vineyard conditions, can add unique dimensions to certain wines. Sauternes, Beerenauslese and Tokaji owe much of their fame and character to this fungus.

spitting your wine all over someone or something. Experience is the only teacher. The best way I can describe it is whistling backwards. Of course, if you can't whistle frontwards you may have another problem on your hands.

At any rate, I'd suggest you practice with water or very cheap wine until you can do it reasonably well. Even though you may need a bib for the first few attempts the dividends are well worth the effort.

And don't worry about the propriety of it all. In wine circles it's common, even anticipated. However, on occasions other than formal wine tastings do make sure those in your company know what you're doing lest they interpret your actions as a form of indecent behavior.

TACTILE

As our organeleptic examination continues, two **tactile** (touch) sensations now deserve our attention. Your tongue is the major instrument used to make determinations for both points, **Body** and **Astringency.**

Body

Here is one of the most difficult sensory assessments to make. Difficult because words fail to describe this sensation satisfactorily. So if you feel a trifle wanting at the end of this section don't be too surprised. And I wouldn't recommend that you start an exhaustive search for more information; there's precious little to be had on this point anywhere.

Alcohol (ethanol), glycerine and to some extent residual sugars, are the components that create the feeling of **body** in wine. Without them the wine would be watery, exhibiting a very *thin* consistency. The opposite, a wine with good body would be termed *full.*

Viscosity is another word that helps us appreciate what is meant by body. Think of water and heavy cream. Their textures are quite descriptive of *thin* and *full* bodied. Alcohol content ranges from 7-14% for table wines and 14-20% for fortified (distilled spirits added) wine. Glycerine, usually formed during fermentation, can vary due to the length of fermentation but ranges usually between 6-10 grams per litre. However, grapes that have been affected by *noble rot* (a bene-

Tears or Legs give a visual clue to the body or texture of the wine.

ficial mold) can impart additional glycerine to the wine sometimes creating 10 or more grams per litre even before fermentation.

But we must ask, is being full bodied always a merit and anything less, respectively negative?

For certain wines, yes! For others, definitely not! And here you thought this was going to be simple and straightforward.

A very full bodied dry Riesling or Chardonnay table wine, in most cases, would be indicative of a poorly *balanced* wine. Wines produced from famous red grapes like Syrah (Rhone), Nebbiolo (Barolo), Pinot Noir (Burgundy) and the Cabernet Sauvignon (grown in California) as contrasting examples, are expected to be wines that are more full bodied in style.

Dessert wines, high in sugar, fortified with alcohol, or just having a naturally high alcohol level would be deserving of the term **heavy** in connection with their body. For table wines heavy would most often represent an imbalance.

If I can turn your attention back to your eyes for just a moment or so we can consider one added element which will aid you to more fully evaluate this factor of body. **Legs!** We can only examine the legs or **tears** of a wine visually, so we have no choice but to abandon the tongue momentarily. We could have discussed this point along with the other Visual aspects but I felt it more apropriate to wait until we reached Body. After all, it's easier to refer back to something you've already read than forward to an unknown.

Legs or *tears*, either term is suitable, are those clear little rivulets that frequently roll down the side of your glass, after the wine has been swished around a bit. (see the photograph on page 64) They are created by the alcohol and glycerine in the wine and provide you with a visual indication of the texture or body of that wine.

It's not the size or number of these legs that's significant but the time before two or more tears formulate, become visible, and begin to slide down the side of the glass. Wines very low in alcohol and glycerine sheet off the glass very quickly with perhaps only tiny droplets remaining, but no legs. It's hard to get around that way, even for a wine, and obviously it's the mark of a very *thin* wine. The longer it takes to form the legs the more significant the body.

Astringency

A sensation that is very frequently confused with bitterness is the second of our Tactile factors, **Astringency**. Although it, as well as Bitterness, originate from the same wine components (poly-phenolics or tannins) *bitterness* is a true, taste sensation while *astringency* is tactile, related to touch.

You should have little difficulty identifying it. It leaves a rough, gritty feeling on your tongue, teeth and on the inside of your cheeks. A wine without an appreciable level of tannin, thus virtually no astringency, would be described as *smooth*. When tannins become very evident they call for descriptions like *harsh, hard,* and *green*. If you've ever had a cup of tea that has steeped too long on the leaves you will have some idea of this quality.

Red wines have by nature more tannins (from their skins) and are therefore expected, early in their life, to be more astringent than whites. This single element accounts for much of the reason why reds generally look forward to longer lives than whites. The tannins that cause astringency act as a natural preservative.

In assessing its overall value to a wine, once more we're dealing with a two-edged sword. Generally, if a white wine is even mildly astringent, much longer than six months or a year it will generally indicate a fault and should be rated that way. But for red wines a very different scenario is enacted.

Early in its life most red wines should have a respectable level of tannin and be noticeably astringent. If you know it to be a young wine then this will be a positive factor for that wine, for the astringency can be a promise of good years ahead. Again, you have to evaluate the wine for what it is now and with all that youthful astringency it is not in the most pleasant shape for consumption. So you rate it for now, noting that it will improve gaining in points as well as stature. But as the wine ages the tannins begin to *drop out* and the wine softens with each birthday reaching an ideal stage where it is no longer an astringent wine, but smooth and silky. At least that's the way the scene should play for fine and great wines.

However, if this does not occur, this softening with age, I'm afraid you'll have to count it as a negative. The rate at which a wine softens, with respect to its tannins, will be unique to that wine and that vintage.

However, when it becomes obvious that the wine will improve no longer and is indeed deteriorating in several other respects, with yet a pronounced astringency, the future of this *poor* wine has all but run its course.

The late Sam Sebastiani was a renowned winetaster and winemaker in the Sonoma region of California.

M. Francoise Bouchard tastes one of his famed Burgundy jewels.

A Matter of Taste 5

TASTE

True, we've been talking about *taste* all along. But finally we're ready to consider, not the broad sense of the word, but the three more specific true, **taste** functions differentiated solely by your tongue. These are the sensations we earlier identified as *sweetness, acidity* (sourness), and *bitterness.*

However, in advance of tackling these three elements, one at a time, it's the ideal time for us to consider very briefly the word threshold. You have many, you know.

There's your threshold of hearing, the point at which you can no longer hear a sound. For the average person their hearing threshold is approximately 50 cycles on the low end to 15,000 cycles on the high end. Beyond either threshold sounds are audible only to the exceptional human ear.

You have a personal threshold of pain too, a threshold most of us don't really care to experiment with, not even in the interest of science. These two rather simple examples help us appreciate that each person's threshold varies for every sensation. This is also true for all the different sensory stimulations we've discussed to this point and for the ones yet to come.

For each odor, for each taste, and for each sensation of touch, you have a personal threshold, a point beyond which you lose the ability to sense that particular stimulant. One winelover may be able to sense even minute traces of sweetness but be almost *dumb* when it comes to reacting to all but major doses of different acids, let's say. The complete opposite could be true for another taster.

A few simple taste experiments contained in Chapter VIII will help you determine if you have a threshold that will act as a serious impediment to your judging wine fairly accurately. Most of us don't, but should one become evident you can simply make use of a friend who doesn't have that particular drawback.

Finding a group of wineloving friends whose strengths and weaknesses inter-relate, compensating for each other, can be fun and rewarding. By combining your strengths in a composite rating your accuracy and consistency will be greatly improved. Professional tasting panels often function in just this manner.

Sweetness

This factor alone causes more differences of opinion than perhaps all the other factors which determine the quality of a wine, grouped together. It seems most persons are quite adamant about their personal preferences when it comes to sweetness. So much so that this offers for us a major hurdle to surmount. It's "one teaspoon of sugar in my tea and that's it! I'll never change" type of attitude we're faced with. Far too often it's this strong preference which clouds judgments. So if the sugar content of a wine is not in tune with their personal taste the rating of that wine could suffer as a whole.

It's a tough tendency to overcome, especially for new winedrinkers and I have no easy formula for defeating it. At least, to be forewarned is to be forearmed, or something like that.

What seems to further complicate this situation, sweetness levels do not dogmatically define a virtue or a fault. Much depends on the type of wine and what the winemaker was trying to accomplish in the first place and how this quality relates to other facets of the wine. There was a time when you could list varieties of grapes, related to a region, and arbitrarily state that wines made from them should ideally have only a specific sweetness. And few authorities in this field would disagree.

It's no longer that simple. Producers around the world do experiment with consumer preferences by producing wines from the same grapes with different residual sugar levels. Even some traditional wine producers from the traditional wine regions are finding that if they are going to sell their product on the international market they are pressured by the complexity of that market to alter their products to meet a variety of local taste preferences, especially where sweetness is concerned.

With red table wines we are still primarily talking about wines that are normally quite *dry*. Only occasionally do we see red table wines coming to market with a touch of sugar (1-2%). For these wines, quite often the term **Mellow** will be marked on their labels to identify this characteristic.

Sweetness has traditionally been, and continues to be, more pertinent to white wines and rosés. Millions have taken their first step into the wonderful world of wine in just the past decade or so. And it's been white wines and rosés, because of their simpler nature and broader sweetness range, that have been the bridge with which many make that transition from other alcoholic beverages to the wine world.

Individuals vary considerably in their sweetness thresholds, their ability to detect sugars. The average threshold is about 1% sugar. Any less and for most of us the sugar seems to disappear all together.

We find two natural sugars in wine, glucose and fructose. There are more but these two are by far the most significant. Interestingly, we are all more sensitive to fructose than to glucose.

And just about the time you're telling yourself you're a pretty good judge of sweetness and that assessing sugar content in wine should be fairly simple, consider this, before you take any bows. Several constituents in wine create the illusion of sweetness, while other elements will confuse your ability to judge the legitimate sugar level accurately.

Alcohol, glycerol, butanediol and certain yeasts can actually make you think you are sensing a certain level of sugar. And it's the acidity, astringency, and bitterness that can seriously confuse your awareness of sugar levels. If, for example, the wine is overly tart or even bitter, will you be able to accurately judge the degree of sugar, in comparison to a wine of equal sugar content but having little tartness or bitterness? These and other elements can mask or enhance your perception of sweetness. But don't be disheartened. It may be a little difficult at first but with some practice it's far from impossible. (see chapter VIII for some exercises that will help)

About this time you're probably wondering, where does all this residual sugar come from? Doesn't all the natural grape sugar get processed, used up, during fermentation, like I've been told?

Most frequently for table wine, yes! All the natural sugars are normally transformed to alcohol and CO_2 (carbon dioxide) during fermentation, leaving us with a totally dry wine. But several doors are open to the modern winemaker to arrest fermentation at various points, leaving natural, residual sugars to act as sweetners.

The most natural method of accomplishing this is simply to use grapes with super amounts of sugar in them. During fermentation the yeasts and sugars start making alcohol. But yeast is a little human in one respect, it can stand only so much alcohol. When the new wine achieves a certain level of alcohol (10-14%) the remaining yeast cells just roll over and die, so to speak, and the wine stops fermenting. But because of using these super-sweet grapes you'll end up with sugar left over and a wine with a certain degree of sweetness.

This can only be carried so far. Many grapes that do produce high levels of sugar do not produce wines of quality. But there are some grapes that are late-picked (therefore developing additional sugar content) and are super-ripened to the point they have so much residual sugar they produce true dessert wines naturally (Sauternes, Beerenausleses, Tokays, etc.)

But how do you get any residual sugar from grapes having only normal sugar levels and when all you want is a touch of sweetness left in the wine? Modern technology has the answer, several in fact.

With modern equipment, especially filters and centrifuges, fermentation can now be halted at almost any point. First you select the desired alcohol/residual sugar ratio and when that point is reached during fermentation the wine is then centrifuged and/or filtered removing the remaining live yeast cells. You are then left a wine with the exact balance you want. At the same time though, the wine could be lacking in any number of other desirable characteristics.

This is obviously a gross oversimplification of the whole procedure, as there are innumerable factors and technicalities that a professional winemaker must evaluate before taking any of these steps. But for our purposes it gives us an overview of what can take place.

Descriptively, you could use terms that range from *dry*, to *medium-dry*, to *medium-sweet*, to *very sweet* to describe residual sugar levels. Some wine authorities use different terms to express the same sensations but those selected are as descriptive as any.*

Notable by its absence in these pages is any consideration of extra or additional sugar being added to wine (chaptalization). To get into this discussion would take too many pages and perhaps be more confusing than enlightening. For our purpose perhaps it will suffice to simply say that for table wines sugar is added from outside sources only when there is a legitimate need, such as when the grapes fail to produce enough natural sugar. Sugar is not added to sweeten the wine. And basically, any sugar that is added (cane sugar usually) is done so during fermentation to aid in the production of proper alcohol levels. The cane sugar *inverts* during the process so essentially acts as would natural fruit sugars.

Acidity

That's the *pucker power*, the *zing* in wine, that *tartness* that gives the wine a certain crispness and bite to it. Without discernable quantities of acid the wine would be the opposite, *dull, flat, insipid*. Both extremes are negative factors. A healthy balance is what we're looking for.

In laboratory language acidity is called *sourness*. It's an unfortunate choice of words since sour has come to mean a spoiled wine in the language of the grape. Oh well, some day that universal wine language . . .

* *Some day there will come to be a universal set of wine terms; at least then wine authorities will have a better idea of what each other is talking about. That alone could be a startling revelation.*

Acidity, or the lack of it, is usually more important to white wines. That's not to suggest it makes no difference at all to red wines, it does. But because whites have fewer tannins, as well as fewer of several other constituents, acids are more significant to the overall character of white wines.

The youthful roughness and harshness of a wine is frequently the result of the stronger, more active nature of that wine's *tartaric* acid. However, with age some of the tartaric acid transforms into insoluable potassium bitartrate and drops out (precipitates) as those tiny, harmless crystals we spoke of earlier.

But wouldn't you know it, there are more acids to consider than just tartaric (is nothing ever simple anymore?). The principal wine acids are Tartaric, Malic, Lactic, Citric, Acetic, and Succinic. They too can influence your judgments.

To get a more complete understanding of the role acid plays there is need to introduce, and briefly explain, four different wine terms used in connection with acid levels . . . *fixed* acidity, *volatile* acidity, *total* acidity, and *real* acidity. It's to your benefit to know the differences.

Fixed Acidity is defined as the combination of all the normal organic, fruit acids found in the grape and subsequently in the wine (acids like tartaric, malic, lactic, citric, etc.).

Volatile Acidity is a technical term which describes acids that can be removed by distillation. For our purposes we are only concerned with one acid that falls into this category — *acetic* acid (vinegar).

Total Acidity is the overall acidity. It's the fixed acidity plus the Volatile Acidity and is frequently the acid count given for wines as so many grams per 100 cc or per litre.

Real Acidity is the term that expresses the wine's **pH** factor (acid/alkaline balance). In case you're not up to date with your shampoo commercials, 7 is neutral pH, below 7 is acidic, above 7 alkaline.

The pH factor for table wines normally varies from about 2.7 to 3.9. All wine is of course acidic (below 7 pH). An extremely tart wine could rate about 2.7 while 3.9 would be very dull and flat, a *flabby* wine. The balance we're looking for, as I'm sure you've already guessed, is somewhere between these two extremes.

In terms of *Total Acidity* a well-balanced wine has approximately 4-8 grams of acid per litre of wine (gram = 1/28th of an ounce).

Bitterness

This factor is frequently confused with *astringency*. That's only fair to state since we said the opposite under the heading of Astringency. In case you missed it the first time, both *bitterness* and *astringency* originate from the same compounds (polyphenolics or tannins). Astringency is a tactile sensation while bitterness is a true, taste stimulation.

One of the first things we should realize about **bitterness** is the difficulty we have in properly describing it. You sense it best on the rear, upper surface of your tongue and it's more prominent in the *finish* or *aftertaste* of the wine, where it is one of the properties that seems to linger awhile on the palate.

Bitterness can be quite normal for a short time in many very young wines. But for sound, well-made white wines it should disappear soon after bottling. For reds it may take a year or so to lose this quality. If it doesn't it will probably remain somewhat bitter for the better part of that wine's lifespan and forever stamp it with at least one negative quality.

A very faint touch of bitterness is characteristic of some red wines and there are those authorities who feel this is not a fault. But it should be so faint you would perhaps have to taste the wine twice to notice it. Anything more and we're back to our negative considerations.

Some white wines, known to be low in tannins, have still exhibited a certain bitterness to them. Why, is yet a mystery to be unravelled. Even though we don't have the answer it still remains a negative when it does appear. White wines that are fermented too long on the skins can also have a bitterness about them as do wines with a high sulphate content. For reds, low acid can also reveal a bitterness.

You would describe a wine, in terms of bitterness, as having *no bitterness,* to being *very bitter.* You can fill in the middle graduations with your own expressions.

As we said, some wine authorities and connoisseurs appreciate a touch of bitterness in certain types of wine, usually reds. But generally it is not a positive factor, even less so with whites. And very definitely it's a fault if there is sufficient bitterness to remind you of caffeine or quinine.

The famed California winemakers Ernest and Julio Gallo.

Getting It All Together 6

To this point we've examined in detail separate wine factors to determine their individual merits and what they add to or take away from the quality of the wine. The next five facets deal with aspects of how well a number of these elements combine or *marry*. If some elements, even in a fine wine, are at odds with each other the wine as a whole suffers. Yet, wines that may be quite ordinary by nature could have their component parts so well in tune with each other they give to the drinker a very pleasurable overall experience. Such a wine would be called *harmonious*.

FLAVOUR

It's a rather awkward quality to put into words. Technically, it is defined by some as *in-mouth odors*, the taste assessment of the factors you first judge with your nose. But actually much more is involved.

We've already examined individually several *flavor factors* with our nose and tastebuds. But under this heading of **flavor** we attempt to interrelate all these constituents, arriving at a general impression which defines that wine's flavor. Here the nose and taste functions work as a team, in tandem, complimenting each other, the sum greater than the parts, a kind of *synergistic* function. Neither the nose nor our sense of taste can individually master this depth of stimulation. They must collaborate.

One of the most important elements contributing to our appraisal of flavor is what wine connoisseurs call **finish**. They're talking about that lingering, overall characteristic impression left by the flavor. A wine with a poor finish (after-taste) will be short-lived in your mouth, its impression fading quickly once it is swallowed.

Our ideal is a comfortable, lengthy reminder of the composite character of the flavor. Just the opposite, is a wine with a *short finish*, the flavor disappearing quickly. However, should it linger too long, wearing out its welcome, this too would be a fault, every bit as negative as if it disappeared before you had a chance to really get to know it.

Some experts suggest the length of the flavor impression should last so many seconds precisely and you should count this off in seconds to determine this factor. If you choose to do so give yourself considerable latitude as there are any number of factors that can affect the consistency of such a practice. Make sure what you're sensing is not lingering bitterness, tannins, acid or sweetness. They may all individually linger longer than the true composite flavor.

TYPICALNESS

This word upsets some wine authorities considerably. They quite rightly feel that the word is abused and that you cannot *stamp out* wines as if using a cookie-cutter. Each wine is an individual.

Though I agree with them in principle I still feel the judicious use of this term is justified. It can help you become a better judge of wines, if used in proper perspective. You are however, cautioned against misuse of the word, trying to fit wines into slots they don't really belong. A good example . . . those who insist on comparing the fine Cabernet Sauvignon varietals of California with the noble red Bordeaux wines of France. This can be a fascinating challenge but too often some non-qualitative (typical) factors are allowed to reflect in the judging procedure. In many non-qualitative respects the two wines can be very different and comparisons on this basis can be unfair to both. It's a pity to see so many get caught in this trap, even professionals, who should know better do so on occasion. I reluctantly include myself in this group.

Essentially, *typicalness* is a touchstone, a reference point. When the grape variety is known there are certain basic (our apple vs. orange) qualities that should be apparent. This reference point helps us to relatively evaluate wines made from the same grape variety, but grown in different regions, for example. I use the term *relatively* because certain grapes develop markedly different characteristics when grown in different regions, characteristics that are not necessarily related to quality. There are still a number of factors that can be legitimately compared, but you should limit it to these.

Most importantly, this *standard*, if I can use that term, becomes valuable when judging different vintages from a known region and/or producer. They certainly should possess many *typical* qualities.

However, when you're judging *non-descript* wines (wines made from non-distinctive grape varieties) *typicalness* becomes almost impossible, as a factor, to apply, except in the most general terms.

It's also under this heading I would like to have you consider all those bubbles found in sparkling wines. This characteristic is one that must certainly be considered typical for specific wines.

By delaying our consideration of carbonation until this point you've been, in a way, forced to look past the fizz of a sparkling or crackling wine to its many other merits. And I feel this is an important point, too often overlooked with such wines. A fine Champagne for example, with or without its famous bubbles, is still a **fine** wine.

There are three basic methods you can employ to make a wine *sparkle* or *crackle*. The cheapest and fastest method is simply to inject the wine with CO_2 (carbon dioxide gas) as they do with soda pop. The bubbles are characteristically large and coarse in a *tactile* and *visual* sense. Wines made in this fashion are usually cheap to start with and the sparkle flattens fairly quickly.

Charmat Methode or Cuvee Close is the phrase used to describe a bulk fermentation system that creates sparkling wines in large closed tanks. The bottling is then done under pressure. Wines made with this

Jean-Marc Charles Heidsieck of the famous Champagne family pours a glass of his renowned "bubbly". The creamy 'head' is one mark of the true "Methode Champenoise."

process are better than those injected with CO_2 gas but I've come across few appraisals for this method, from any wine authorities, that could be called glowing. The subsequent filtering these wines receive before bottling can remove some of the sparkle, causing the wine to flatten sooner.

The superior method, recognized unanimously as such, is the **Methode Champenoise**. This age old process employs a second, individual bottle fermentation. It takes longer, is more expensive, but the results are well worth it all.

On pouring a glass of sparkling wine made from this process (many wines other than Champagne use it) you will immediately note two Visual characteristics that often separate it from the imitators. First, you will notice that after the first layer of foam has died away a tenacious collar of tiny bubbles will often remain around the edge of the wine next to the glass. It should become apparent the bubbles themselves are different, too. They are smaller, fine bubbles that appear slowly and last longer than either of the other two processes, especially when compared to the wines that are artificially gassed.

Now if we could just convince some governments that bubbles in wine do not constitute a legitimate reason for an added levy of tax . . .

BALANCE

This is a quality desirable for all wines . . . from the most humble *vin du pays* to those which aspire to greatness. It is the term used to describe how well the component parts of the wine ultimately *harmonize* or *marry*.

For a wine to possess **Balance** all the individual elements will be in *tune* with each other, allowing even **ordinary** wines to demonstrate this virtue. So, a wine that exhibits a fine *nose* but has poor *taste* qualities would be assessed as **un**balanced. Consideration, however must be given to that wine's maturity, for a wine may take several years, even decades, to achieve this balance or harmony.

Of course, you will have to score it for what degree of balance it demonstrates at the moment, if you're doing an evaluation. This leaves room for that score to increase if indeed the wine's balance does improve.

GENERAL QUALITY

When we reach this heading we've come full circle. For the past 80 pages or more we've been inviting you to carefully dissect a wine step-by-step. Now, we're asking you to put it all back together and assess it as a single entity.

The *overall* impression you receive, swallowing more of the wine at this point, will relate the total richness of the wine's character. In a sense it's the *marriage* of all those points we've considered individually . . . the appearance, the color, aroma, bouquet, the three true taste sensations, etc. How does the wine affect you? Is it a memorable wine?

You are tasting the wine as a *single entity* now, assessing its character as an individual wine. You may even discover that two faults you had previously identified could, in effect, cancel each other out, by acting as a counter-balance to each other (acid/sugar excesses) producing a wine that is generally very pleasant.

So, this is not a regressive step but a final and necessary component of your total evaluation. But take care not to use this category to correct previous individual evaluations or to express your personal likes and dislikes. If need be, go back and alter your first impression if you have modified your judgment on a certain point. As stated earlier, evaluating or judging wine is not a contest. It's an honest attempt to understand and accurately assess the merits of a wine.

HEDONIC

If you want another way to express how much *pleasure* you derive from something, **Hedonic** is not a bad word to use.

Since it seems an impossibility for any member of our human family to be totally objective my purpose for introducing a Hedonic factor to your evaluations is an attempt to at least contain this element, as much as possible, to one section of the rating process.

There are any number of environmental influences which play a part in creating a person's individual taste. Cultural, family and religious are but a few of the more obvious influences. So this is the place to express them. You've been struggling to remain as objective as possible to this point, now's the time to let it all out. You're encouraged to express a flat out *like* or *dislike* opinion. Be opinionated . . . just don't let your previous, more critical analysis influence the expression of your *gut* feelings.

Some *taste* experts will object to the inclusion of such a **Hedonic** factor in the wine evaluation process. If it bothers anyone that much, ignore it.

Roger Lenique former Chef de Caves for the well-known Taittinger Champagne House.

Putting It Into Practice 7

THE SETTING

Depending on the type of wine tasting you desire at the time, the setting, your tasting environment, may strongly influence your wine judging abilities.

If your wine tasting affair is more casual by nature, a few friends and a few bottles of wine, a wine *sampling* more than a *tasting*, you may not desire to be all that critical. And there's nothing wrong with this arrangement. In fact it can be very enjoyable, just getting to know a little more about a few wines and a few friends, in a more relaxed and casual atmosphere. It's a legitimate type of wine tasting that is rewarding and satisfying in a way no professional tasting could be.

But if you're looking for a more practical, learning experience, perhaps even keeping a record of your ratings, you will want to pay a little more attention to detail. We spoke earlier of outside influences that could alter your judgments. Lighting, background color, sound, all can have a distinct affect on your sensory impressions.

First, the lighting. If it's completely impractical for you to provide indirect, natural lighting (an evening tasting is a good reason) the best alternative is clear, incandescent bulbs. Small desk or student type lamps equipped with such bulbs, sans any frosted covers, are excellent for this purpose. They will influence the natural wine color the least. Most fluorescent lighting will not only alter your color judgments but they can, quite surprisingly, distort your sense of taste, too. So do stay away from them.

If your private, little get-together includes food before or after the tasting be sure there are no strong prevailing odors in the room (foods like kippers and boiled cabbage are definite offenders). Some odors more than others can adversely confuse your sensory abilities. It may, depending on the situation, be necessary to deodorize the room with a neutral scent.

Since its been claimed that music can soothe the savage beast it shouldn't be all that surprising that it has the power to influence your wine ratings. This has been well documented and the effect is quite consistent. So turn off the stereo and politely remind your more vociferous co-tasters to *belt up* during the actual tasting. Even casual remarks can throw you off.

"Oh, isn't that marvelous George!" has got to start you wondering which point was so marvelous. Your objectivity can go out the window with one simple comment.

No Smoking! Post this sign prominently and don't shy away from reminding offenders. As little as two cigarettes smoked in a closed, average-sized room is sufficient to distort both visual and olfactory senses significantly. If someone can't possibly go that long without a *butt* serve them a glass of Scotch and ask him or her to do whatever it is they have to do in another room. This is not intended to offend any smoker. As an ex-smoker I can't recall ever taking offence at *no smoking* regulations at a wine tasting; it's the expected thing. Not only is it expected but it is only reasonable and considerate.

Try to provide as white a background as possible (walls, tablecloth, etc.). Your room's color scheme may be the talk of the decorating set but it could seriously upset your color and taste judgments. So do your best in this respect.

Schenley wine salesmen attend a wine school conducted by the author. Such classes stress the Art of tasting wine from a very objective point of view.

Wineries arrange for tastings of their new wines on a regular basis as this German producer does for his many varieties and vintages.

Glasses should be uncolored, crystal clear, and minus any of those lovely cut-glass patterns. They should be large enough (holding 6-10 ozs.), stemmed, (to keep your fingerprints off the bowl) and tulip-shaped (the opening smaller than the bowl) which acts to funnel the aroma and bouquet to your nose.

When washing your glasses, in preparation for the tasting, make certain to rinse them thoroughly several times. Dry and polish them with a lint-free cloth (linen, etc.). Some authorities prefer to air-dry their glasses after the final rinse. The purpose of all this fuss is to ensure there will be no taste or smell from residual detergent or soap. Some experts even go to the point of rinsing their glasses only in distilled water to avoid odors from some of the chemicals in tap water. If you use an automatic dishwasher, **BEWARE** of dishwasher detergents. That ingredient that makes the water *sheet* off the glasses so nicely, avoiding all those spots, can remain to create off odors and tastes. If you can, put the glasses through a couple of extra rinse cycles, minus the soap or rinse agents.

When you find yourself running short of glasses and it's not all that practical to wash and dry them between samples there is an alternative solution. Pour a half an ounce or so of the next wine to be tasted into the used glass, swish it around and pour it out. The glass is now ready for that wine to be sampled. Of course, you'll have to calculate if the wine loss is significant enough at some point to justify the purchase of additional glasses.

And don't overdo it, please. Professionals are accustomed to tasting twenty, thirty, forty, fifty or more wines at a sitting without becoming inundated or inebriated. Try to keep your sampling down to four to eight wines at the most, for one event. Not only can it be less expensive but the impression and insight you do get from one wine will not then be washed away in a tide of too many samples. One of our objectives is to build a taste memory, not to set a world's record for the most wines tasted in one sitting.

The suggested order of tasting is fairly straightforward . . . whites before rosés, rosés before reds, and dry before sweet. To avoid the tired old cracker versus cheese versus French bread debate (as devices to clear the palate between wines) provide your tasters with room temperature distilled water and separate glasses. It works best. And don't forget a bucket for expelling the wine. If you don't have an official spittoon-type bucket for this purpose anything that's visually not too unattractive and doesn't leak will do. You may also want to provide your tasters with some type of evaluation sheet. While some might prefer to simply rank the wines for that tasting, that can be a bit shallow when compared to a rating of the wines.

The advantage of using one of the rating systems is your ability to relate the ratings from one tasting, to wines scored at another tasting, weeks, months, even years apart. Simply *ranking* a series of wines at one tasting, from the best to the worst may indeed have some value, if that's what you want to do. But that fails you as a taster when you desire to relate those wines to anything outside of that particular tasting event.

An Evaluation system, to work to your ultimate benefit, must disclose to you, the taster, the essence, the nature, the stature, the intrinsic value of every wine, regardless of when or with which wines it was tasted. Each wine should be approached and assessed as an individual, and should be evaluated in relationship to consistent rating systems — **not** another wine.

THE CHARTS

So much for theory! Choose your system and taste on!

For any system to work dependably it should induce you to follow a natural step-by-step, objective method of evaluation. Make sure it does and that it does not leave broad areas open to a single assessment, such as assigning 30 or 40 points out of 100 to a single factor or jump back and forth between nose, tactile and taste functions.

On pages 93-99 you will again see a number of sample charts, some of the most popular in use today. There are obviously a number of significant differences.

It's not my purpose to pit these charts against each other. They're different and purposely so. For classroom purposes I use the chart represented on page 99. Why a 100-point scoring system in contrast to the more popular 20-point rating system? In general terms, a score out of 100 is easier for most persons to relate to. Sixteen points out of 20 is

Appearance — evaluating the *surface* condition and *clarity* of the wine. Any single, major fault should cause you to rate it 1 (Poor). Two significant faults, 0 (Bad). No faults and a *brilliant*, crystal-clear appearance, score it 4 (Great). Fault free and just *bright*, 3 points (Fine). If the wine was not bright and clear but on the dull side, 2 points and if it were otherwise fault free but a bit *hazy*, 1 point would be all that it rates. *Cloudy*, 0.

Intensity — prominence of composite wine odors. Clean, vinuous, characteristic, very *intense* and pleasant, score 4. No faults with a good strong nose, score 3. *Light*, pleasant nose, counts 2. Elusive but vinous smell, give it 1. Non-existent or offensive odor, 0.

Aroma — smell of the *fruit*, the grape itself. You must consider the age of the wine, as aroma declines to become part of and all but disappearing in the bouquet. A prominent, characteristic, easily identifiable, varietal aroma that is appropriate for its age, score it 4. Distinctive, fresh aroma, in keeping with its age and grape variety counts 3. Aromatic, but not distinctive enough to determine the grape parentage, mark it 2. Elusive, non-descript aroma scores 1. Totally inappropriate for age or a non-existent aroma calls for a 0.

Bouquet — odors created by the *vinification* and *ageing* of the wine. As the wine ages this will include the varietal character of the aroma. No major faults gets the wine at least a score of 2. If the bouquet has complexity (from ageing odors) is clean and pleasant, add another point. If it literally fills your nostrils with a wonderful, *complex* and *lasting fragrance*, give it the highest marks. With each major fault it drops a point below 2, if it has no other outstanding attributes.

Body — *texture* or *consistency* appropriate to that wine type. Review carefully the information under this heading on pages Since much of the body originates with the alcohol content check the alcohol level (on the label if possible). Also, check the *legs* of the wine. Keep in mind grape variety will tell you whether the wine should be full, a big wine, or not. The other factor causing a wine to have more or less body is *residual sugar* content. It should be in keeping with the type of wine. Each step away from the ideal texture of a *velvety smooth* consistency drops the score 1 point.

Astringency — *tactile* sensation originating with the wine's tannins. There is a natural development from a rough feeling in its youth to silk-like texture that comes during maturity. So you must relate this factor to the wine's age. When you've determined how much astringency should exist for this wine, considering its type and age, factor to the wine's age. Although the existence of tannins may indicate a promising future you must score it for what it is now. That's for reds.

For white wines a slight astringency may be evident in youth but that should quickly disappear. If it doesn't start lopping off points.

Color — assessing the *tint* (hue) and *depth* (density) of the wine's color. When both factors are ideal, taking into consideration its age, score 4. When one or the other is slightly off, count 3. Proper color but lacking significant depth, score it 2. Both factors less than appropriate, score 1. Wrong or exaggerated shades, 0.

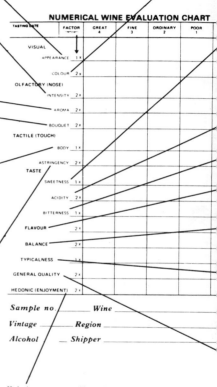

NUMERICAL WINE EVALUATION CHART

TASTING DATE	FACTOR	GREAT 4	FINE 3	ORDINARY 2	POOR 1
VISUAL					
	APPEARANCE 1x				
	COLOUR 2x				
OLFACTORY (NOSE)					
	INTENSITY 2x				
	AROMA 2x				
	BOUQUET 2x				
TACTILE (TOUCH)					
	BODY 1x				
	ASTRINGENCY 2x				
TASTE					
	SWEETNESS 1x				
	ACIDITY 2x				
	BITTERNESS 1x				
	FLAVOUR 2x				
	BALANCE 2x				
	TYPICALNESS 1x				
GENERAL QUALITY 2x					
HEDONIC (ENJOYMENT) 2x					

Sample no. _____ *Wine* _____

Vintage _____ *Region* _____

Alcohol _____ *Shipper* _____

Hedonic — your personal impression; the amount of *pleasure* you receive from this wine; a straightforward expression of *like* or *dislike*. Now's the time to let whimsy reign. Only you can tell how much the wine pleases you.

The overriding factor that must be considered at this point — any single score falling into the "Bad" category may well in itself be sufficient to totally discredit the wine. For example, a wine which scores "0" in the acid column, because of too much acetic acid (vinegar), may be sufficient to fault the wine totally regardless of the other ratings.

Using this or any system, water could theoretically score at least a few points (for clarity, etc.). So any evaluation system has to be kept in context — understanding that a major fault or shortcoming could nullify any rating.

Sweetness — the level of *residual* sugars. Again, this quality is appropriate to a particular wine type. If it demonstrates the ideal level of discernable sweetness, not being offensively dry either, for that type of wine, mark it 4. If the wine is obviously far too sweet or dry for the type or the acid level it counts 0. You will have to assess the intermediates accordingly.

Acidity — the quality which gives a wine its *crisp, tart* taste. If there is no discernable *acetic* acid (vinegar) taste start your scoring at 2. If you suspect there is a touch of acetic acid or the wine is completely *dull* or *flat* (too little acid) mark it 1. If you sense positively a vinegariness mark it 0. When the wine has no acetic acid fault and has a well balanced, pleasant acid content score it 3. And if the wine, again considering its age, is crisp, clean, faultless (and you're in a good mood) give it full marks, 4.

Comments

Bitterness — a *true taste* sensation, better recognized in the *finish*, the after taste. If a wine has matured and a prominent disagreeable bitterness still exists mark it 0, it will never improve. If there is no hint of bitterness, nothing but a characteristic prominent flavor in the after taste, count this as 4. You can grade the intermediates, keeping in mind a natural youthful bitterness that should disappear with age.

Flavor — the *composite* of taste and nose characteristics. If the flavor is barely vinuous (wine like) and disappears as soon as the wine leaves your mouth, score it 1. If recognizable and pleasant and it doesn't die too quickly score it 2. If a faultless flavor lingers pleasantly for a few moments, mark it a 3. But if it persists for some time while demonstrating outstanding qualities, 4 is the score. Don't confuse this with the cloying, overly persistent flavors of some grapes; that's a weakness, an excess. And don't be confused by the lingering astringency or acidity of some wines. These qualities can persist, giving the impression of a nice, lengthy flavor but in fact are not the true flavor.

Balance — the absence of excesses or deficiencies. Even an *ordinary* wine can score well here, if all its qualities are in keeping with its general nature. Simply check back on your score sheet. If to this point your numerical scores are all in one column. (3's for example) the wine is perfectly balanced and deserves a 4. With 1 or 2 marks different it will still deserve a 3. When it has obvious ups and downs (e.g. fine appearance, ordinary nose, poor taste) score it 2. If there are wide discrepancies, 1 is all it deserves and when your scoring is all over the board, extreme to extreme, that's bad and worth the 0 it gets for this.

Typicalness — a reference point; judging with known standards. If the wine meets all fundamental criteria for that variety and type it should receive full marks. For each step away from the standard drop 1 point. Be careful not to impose standards from one region on wines made from the same variety of grapes but from different regions. For a general guide to wine types and grape varieties see Chapter IX.

SCORE
ngs
Great
Fine
inary
oor
eptable

General Quality — the consideration of all components as *one entity*. If the wine is faultless, has a memorable, outstanding nature, is a wine of distinction and of the highest calibre rate it accordingly, 4 points. With one or two minor faults and all its other component parts in *harmony*, this *fine* wine scores 3 points. When several factors are out of place but they are not glaring deficiencies or extremes the wine will be **ordinary**, 2 points. If it is still drinkable and not an unpleasant experience 1 point (poor), is all you can give it. If you find it hard to swallow forget all your calculations, and that wine as well.

Question: where does the **alcohol** in the wine fit into this system's evaluation? *Answer:* in several places.

First: in the bouquet — you will smell the alcohol — it should be neither excessive nor too elusive.

Second: under the *Tactile* heading in your assessment of *body*. It is one of the major factors influencing this point. It also creates a mechanical feeling (Kinesthetic), a burning sensation.

Third: alcohol has a taste, not much, but it does create an impression of *sweetness* — so assessment under this heading is also involved.

Fourth: under *Flavor, General Quality* and *Typicalness* factors it is also a part of your evaluations.

not so quickly understood as it would be if you scored it 80 out of 100. Also, the 100-point system allows us to introduce a number of additional factors like balance, bitterness, etc., which I feel are valuable and necessary inputs to a complete evaluation. And in this "Metric" age a 100 point scale seems justified and somewhat more practical. But each to his own.

There are no scoring systems that will escape the critic's searching eye. All have shortcomings that will be brought to public attention. This chart will not escape that distinctive privilege. But it works reasonably well for personal and instructive use.

SCORING

Until you have all the information in Chapters I to VI reasonably well in mind my suggestion would be to refer back to each factor and the appropriate details before you assign a score to that factor.

As you gain precious experience, each time a particular factor comes to mind you will be able to quickly run a mental check on the points under each heading. But that takes time and practice, so, for the moment make liberal use of the written material.

The previous two pages represent some sample guidelines for using this particular 100-point system. The operative word here is "guidelines". They are not inviolable rules and regulations. But it can present you with a fairly accurate and consistent profile for each wine — not an infallible critique.

SCORE CARD TRANSLATED
FROM THE ASSOCIAZIONE
ENOTECNICI ITALIANI

	Weight	Excellent 4	Good 3	Average 2	Mediocre 1	Bad 0

VISUAL

Appearance   2 _____

Color   2 _____

OLFACTORY

Finesse   2 _____

Intensity   2 _____

Freshness   2 _____

TASTE

Body   2 _____

Harmony   2 _____

Intensity   2 _____

Final taste-odor

sensation   3 _____

Typical   3 _____

General

    Impression   3 _____

Name _____

Date _____

TRANSLATED
FROM THE OFFICE
DE LA VIGNE ET DU VIN
PARIS, FRANCE

Characteristic	Weight	Multiplying factor for increasing defects				
		X0	X1	X4	X9	X16
Appearance	1					
Color	1					
Odor Intensity	1					
Odor Quality	2					
Taste Intensity	2					
Taste Quality	3					
Harmony	2					

Multiplying factors: outstanding (0); very good (1); good (4); acceptable (9); unacceptable (16).

Name _____

Date _____

German Wine Society

DATE ....

WINE ....

VINTAGE .... **GRAPE VARIETY** ....

CLASSIFICATION ....

GROWER/SHIPPER ....

	Points	Characteristic
1. COLOUR		
2. CLARITY		
3. BOUQUET		
4. FLAVOUR		
Total		Notes:

DATE ....

WINE ....

VINTAGE .... **GRAPE VARIETY** ....

CLASSIFICATION ....

GROWER/SHIPPER ....

	Points	Characteristic
1. COLOUR		
2. CLARITY		
3. BOUQUET		
4. FLAVOUR		
Total		Notes:

	Max. Points
1. COLOUR	
white	
a) pale, overcoloured	0
b) light	1
c) typical	2
2. CLARITY	
a) dull	0
b) bright	1
c) brilliant	2
3. BOUQUET	
a) defective	0
b) mute	1
c) clean	2
d) fragrant	3
e) fine and flowery	4
4. FLAVOUR	
a) defective	0
b) neutral	1 – 3
c) clean, but thin	4 – 5
d) balanced	6 – 9
e) ripe and noble	10 – 12

CLASSIFICATION	Min. Points
Qualitätswein b. A.	11
Kabinett	13
Spätlese	14
Auslese	15
Beerenauslese	16
Trockenbeerenauslese	17

20 Point Scoring System
(Modified Davis)

Wine Sample _____ Vintage _____

Tasting Date _____ Sample No. _____

Characteristic	Possible Pts.	Score	Comment
Appearance	(2)	_____	_____
Color	(2)	_____	_____
Aroma & Bouquet	(6)	_____	_____
Total Acidity	(2)	_____	_____
Sweetness	(1)	_____	_____
Body	(1)	_____	_____
Flavor	(2)	_____	_____
Bitterness	(1)	_____	_____
Astringency	(1)	_____	_____
General Quality	(2)	_____	_____

Total _____

17-20 Great, 13-16 Fine, 9-12 Ordinary, 5-8 Poor, 0-4 Unacceptable

NAME _____

WINE _____

DATE _____

	TOTAL SCORE 20	
18 - 20	EXCELLENT	
15 - 17	VERY GOOD	
12 - 14	GOOD	
9 - 11	AVERAGE	
	FAIR	7 - 8
	POOR	4 - 6
	EXTREMELY POOR	1 - 3

SAMPLE NO.	APPEARANCE		BOUQUET AND AROMA	TASTE	OVERALL IMPRESSION	TOTAL SCORE	PREF. (RANK)
	COLOUR 2	CLARITY 2	6	8	2		
CONTROL	1	1	3	4	1	10	

NAME:

YEAR: REGION:

APPEARANCE

		Clear,
Cloudy	Dull	Lively

AROMA

				Extremely
Unpleasant	Nondescript	Clear	Pleasant	Pleasant

Very Sweet	Sweet	Medium Dry	Dry	Very Dry

BODY

Extremely				
Light	Light	Medium	Full	Heavy

Soft		Firm		Harsh

Acid		Balanced		Flabby

				Full-
Unpleasant	Flavorless	Light	Moderate	Flavored

Rough Finish		Mild Finish		Smooth Finish

Fades	Gone within	Lingers up to	Lingers	Lingers
Quickly	5 secs.	1 min.	1–60 min.	+ 1 hour

NOTABLE CHARACTERISTICS:

FOOD/OCCASIONS:

GENERAL COMMENTS:

NUMERICAL WINE EVALUATION CHART

TASTING DATE	FACTOR	GREAT 4	FINE 3	ORDINARY 2	POOR 1	BAD 0	SCORE
VISUAL							
APPEARANCE	1 x						
COLOUR	2 x						
OLFACTORY (NOSE)							
INTENSITY	2 x						
AROMA	2 x						
BOUQUET	2 x						
TACTILE (TOUCH)							
BODY	1 x						
ASTRINGENCY	2 x						
TASTE							
SWEETNESS	1 x						
ACIDITY	2 x						
BITTERNESS	1 x						
FLAVOUR	2 x						
BALANCE	2 x						
TYPICALNESS	1 x						
GENERAL QUALITY	2 x						
HEDONIC (ENJOYMENT)	2 x						

Sample no. _____ *Wine* _____

Vintage _____ *Region* _____

Alcohol _____ *Shipper* _____

TOTAL SCORE

Ratings
86 100 Great
70 85 Fine
50 69 Ordinary
35 49 Poor
0 34 Unacceptable

99

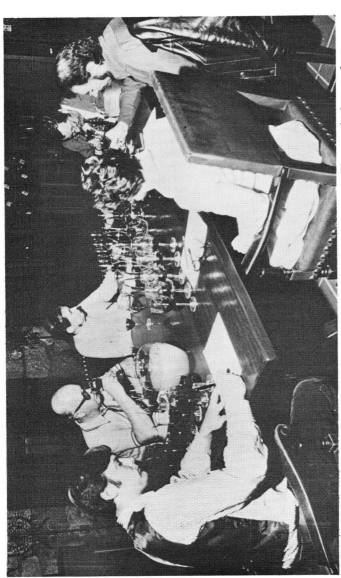

Beaulieu Vineyard tasting panel members evaluate each wine of every vintage throughout its development and residency at the Napa Valley, California winery. This impartial, professional evaluation is a key part of the winemaking process. The panel also conducts comparative blind tastings of vintages from wineries around the world as well as wines of Beaulieu obtained from the BV cellars and from randomly selected retail wine shops.

Tuning Up Your Senses 8

Sensible exercise tones up the muscles, increases your stamina and generally improves your physical well-being. At least that's what it's supposed to accomplish; for some I'm not always certain that's the case.

At any rate, tuning up your senses can be even more rewarding when it comes to wine judging, as there are some very simple, basic exercises well worth the effort.

We are, to a degree, limited in exercises to those that are practical for home experiments.* Color evaluations are limited to our identifying different color intensities, not tints or hues. All the other facets of tasting will have to be gained by direct experience with the wines involved.

I am purposely going to keep this as simple as possible, as much for my benefit as yours.

SWEETNESS

To test and exercise your sensory ability to detect residual sugar levels purchase a dry, red wine that is fairly ordinary in nature, not overly strong in taste or price. You can repeat these tests using similar quality white and rosé wines.

Using granulated cane sugar, dissolve **two** teaspoons in **six** ounces of your selected wine. This will act as your **base** sweetener, so keep it in a separate container.

Now, pour 2 oz. of your selected red wine into four identical glasses. To one glass, add 1 teaspoon of the base sweetener, to the second glass add 2 teaspoons, to the third add 3 teaspoons. The fourth glass remains unadulterated.

At this point mark the glasses in some way to identify which is which, but in a way that is not evident while you are tasting. A simple method is to number pieces of masking tape 0 to 3 and stick them underneath the foot of the glass. Label the pure wine 0 and the others 1 to 3, from the lowest to the greatest amount of added base solution.

Now, have some non-participant in the tasting, while none of the tasters are watching, re-arrange the glasses in a different order. By sampling each you are expected to place the glasses in their respective order of sweetness. From the one with no added sweetener to the sample with three teaspoons of the base sweetener solution. To keep the fluid levels the same in each glass you may find it advantageous to mix up a large *batch* of each solution in a separate container, pouring equal amounts of each into the four glasses.

You can apply the same methodology to *Total Acid, Acetic Acid* (vinegar), and *Tannin* to sharpen your sensory talents for these elements.

ACIDS

To achieve your base solution in a test for Total Acid, dissolve **1/4 teaspoon** of Citric Acid (available at your drugstore) in **5 oz.** of your selected wine. Again, with four sample glasses of wine (2 oz. in each) add 1, 2, and 3 teaspoons to 3 of the glasses, the 4th nothing and repeat your attempts to arrange the glasses in proper order, from no additional acid to highest acid content, by tasting the samples.

To test your sensitivity to Acetic Acid (vinegar) make a base acid solution from **1 tablespoon** of red wine vinegar added to **5 oz.** of wine. Once more, using 4 sample glasses of wine (2 oz. in each) add

1 teaspoon of the base acid solution to one glass, 2 teaspoons to a second, and **4 teaspoons** to the third glass. Now, once more into the breach to see how your senses react.

TANNINS

This test for Tannins has a **CAUTION** to it. Do **NOT** make your base tannin solution for this test too far ahead of time (do it just before the test). Tannic acid can hydrolyze in time to a **TOXIC** acid. A further precaution would be to ask your tasters **not** to **swallow** these samples. If the foregoing hasn't frightened you off, the test goes much the same.

To get your base tannin solution dissolve **1/4 teaspoon** of tannic acid (available at your drugstore) in 9, **repeat 9 oz.** of wine. To the four glasses of wine, this time each having **3 oz.** of wine in them add **1** teaspoon to one glass, **2** to a second, and **4** to the third, the fourth as is, of course.

It becomes very obvious you can alter the selection of these dosed glasses in a variety of ways to make a more complex test. Selecting a sample from each different test *(with the exception of the one for tannin)* to see if you can distinguish which was dosed with which, provides an added challenge. We'll leave all the potential combinations to your imagination and adventuresome spirit.

VISUAL

For a color density test simply cutting the wine with increased amounts of water will give you sufficient exercise in this area.

OLFACTORY

A rather elementary test for *aroma* can be made using *concentrated* apple juice, the type you find in cans in the frozen food section of your supermarket. Using a white wine add 1 teaspoon of undiluted apple concentrate to one glass containing 3 oz. of white wine, 2 to the second and 4 to the third. One glass remains unadulterated, of course. Now, after confusing the order using only your nose, re-arrange them in the correct order from 0-3.

To set up for a *sulphur* test create a *base* solution of water (1litre) to 1/4 tsp. of potassium metabisulphite (available at winemaking supply stores). To glasses with **6 oz** of wine add 1/8 tsp., 1/4 tsp. and 1/2 tsp of the base, one glass at 0, of course. Sniff on!

These exercises will quite definitely tune up your senses and most importantly will give you a better idea of what you are looking for in your normal wine tasting. They can also help you to identify any personal disfunction that would seriously affect your wine tasting endeavours. Quite naturally, depending upon the number of tasters sharing these experiments you'll have to expand your quantity of basic test material.

There are also a number of additional, very simple tests you can set up for yourself and a few wine loving friends. Learning to identify grape variety is one very important exercise.

By purchasing several bottles of varietal wines (wine made primarily from only one variety of grape) like Cabernet Sauvignon, Pinot Noir, Barbera, Merlot, Gamay, Chardonnay, Riesling, Semillon, Sauvignon Blanc, Chenin Blanc, etc., you can group similar types together and practice identifying the individual types.

Label the glasses again, under the foot and have a neutral party arrange the order. From this simple test you will begin to appreciate the qualities that identify the classic wine-making grapes. Be certain to make notes. The same can be done with the superior hybrids like de Chaunac, Marechal Foch, Baco Noir, Villard Noir, Chelois, Verdelet, Aurora, Seyval Blanc, etc.

From this point you can progress to identifying some of the famous wines that are blends of two or more grapes like some of the wines from Bordeaux, Chianti, Chateauneuf du Pape, Cotes du Rhone, Valpolicella, Bardolino, Spain's Rioja wines, Graves, Soave, etc. Then, break them down by countries of origin to see if you can identify certain regional and national characteristics.

Remember, try not to do this alone — invite some friends to join your experiments. It's much more rewarding and pleasant to share the experience. Sharing the cost is not a bad idea either.

With each experiment and each wine your sensitivity and love of good, honest wine will blossom. The dividends are myriad.

The foregoing is not intended to represent an experiment of a laboratory nature. They are simple home experiments designed to test and improve your wine senses.

A Few Grapes And A Little Wine 9

Chapter

An estimated eight thousand grape varieties are currently under cultivation. Less than twenty are considered *classic*.

To attempt to provide a comprehensive description of all these grape varieties and their wines is a monumental, a life-time undertaking. The following guide is obviously not such an attempt. However, to limit our considerations to just those classic jewels of the vineyard would be to shortchange winemaker and winelover alike. So, we have added a few more ordinary but popular types and a special section on **Hybrids**.

Our description of the characteristics for these wines is in the broadest *varietal* terms. Winemakers from region to region often have very different goals in mind when they select a particular grape. And many varieties offer the vintner the needed flexibility to allow them success in a number of directions. So, we must be flexible to the same degree in our judgments.

And neither is this an attempt to establish the 'pecking order' for the top twenty or so winemaking grapes. Many of the wines you will make acquaintance with in the years to come are duly represented here, but not in any suggested or intimated order of merit.

Don't stop here, though. Carry on with your personal wine investigations. Vintage variations, lands of origin, climate, winemaking philosophies, all exercise enough influence on each wine to make it profoundly different.

Get to know as much as possible about each wine you drink by additional reading. You'll be a better judge and a more knowledgeable lover of wine.

VINIFERA WHITE VARIETIES

Grape Variety: Chardonnay
***Wine Colors:** pale yellow/green to yellow
Nose: smokey, fruity bouquet, difficult to describe
Taste: austere, steel-like, dry, rich mineral flavor, nice long finish and pleasant acidity in quality versions – occasionally buttery, nutty
Wines: famed white Burgundies like Chablis, Montrachet, Meursault, etc., varietals
Comments: medium-bodied wines that change character from region to region — not a true Pinot grape — blended with other grapes to produce, real Champagne, Beaujolais Blanc, Macon Blanc and many simple Bourgogne Blancs – popular and excellent varietal in California – grown also in Australia, Canada, New Zealand, Rumania, South Africa, Russia

The normally expected color range influenced by style and/or age.

Grape Variety: Chenin Blanc
Wine Colors: pale yellow/green to pale yellow
Nose: fruity, berry-like aroma, light bouquet
Taste: thirst quenching, fruity and spicy flavor — good sugar/acid balance — both dry and sweeter types – with age, a taste of almonds

Wines:	White wines of Vouvray, Anjou and Saumur in the Loire Valley of France, varietals
Comments:	often a full-bodied wine that does well in cooler climates — when produced by a cold fermentation it creates additional fruitiness — also grown in U.S.A., the Ukraine with small plantings in Australia and New Zealand as well as South Africa

✧

Grape Variety:	Gewurtztraminer
Wine Colors:	pale to medium yellow
Nose:	intense distinctive nose — grapey herb-like aroma — flowery bouquet of roses and jasmine
Taste:	distinctive spicy flavor with a touch of bitterness — soft, velvety and full-bodied — dry to sweet
Wines:	varietal
Comments:	Gewurtztraminer is the more pronounced, distinctive and aromatic strain of the Traminer grape — shows a tendency towards a lower acidity than Riesling but often has some residual sugar — one of the oldest vines known — Alsace sets the standards for this type — known as Tremino Aromatico in Italy, the Formentin in Romania and Hungary and is grown in France, Italy, Germany, Austria, Spain, Australia, New Zealand, Hungary, Romania, U.S.A. and Canada

✧

Grape Variety:	Muller-Thurgau
Wine Colors:	pale yellow to gold
Nose:	clean, fresh, fruity bouquet — spicy, herb-like but not as distinctive as Riesling (see)

Taste: fruity, with a touch of Muscat (see) flavor with a hint of nutmeg — not high in acid, a soft wine — medium to very sweet

Wines: used in many German white wines, blended with other grapes or by itself, varietals

Comments: is now the most widely grown grape in Germany — spreading to Alsace, Switzerland, Italy and England — most probably a self-cross of the White Riesling — does not generally take ageing too well but will improve as a wine as the vines are matched to ideal soils and microclimates

ⅇ

Grape Variety: Muscat Blanc

Wine Colors: pale yellow to gold with occasional greenish tinge

Nose: fruity, musky aroma often related to roses — intense, rich bouquet in some dessert versions

Taste: very pronounced musky flavor, a grapey overall characteristic — from very dry to dessert wines

Wines: Asti Spumante (Italy), Setubal (Portugal), Muscat d'Alsace, and the Muscatels of France, extraordinary Australian dessert versions

Comments: best example of the very large and ancient Muscat family of grapes — makes very dry table wines to quality dessert wines — grown in France, Spain, Portugal, Italy, Africa, Australia, Greece, Russia, U.S.A.

ⅇ

Grape Variety: Pinot Blanc

Wine Colors: pale yellow/green to yellow

Nose:	flowery, fragrant aroma and bouquet, not overly intense
Taste:	subtle but distinct character — vivacious often tannic flavor, very difficult to describe, you'll just have to experience it — dry to sweet
Wines:	varietals, Pinot D'Alsace, Pinot D'Alba and Borgogna Bianco (Italy), blended in some Burgundies and doing well in parts of Germany
Comments:	a mutation of Pinot Noir — grown in most major wine countries — not to be confused with Chardonnay — adapts better to cooler climates — low in acid when grown in warmer regions — smooth, good body, ready soon

∽

Grape Variety:	Pinot Gris
Wine Colors:	pale yellow / green to yellow
Nose:	pleasant, distinctive, flowery aroma and bouquet
Taste:	smooth, fruity taste with slight bitterness in the aftertaste, some claim a hint of almonds — dry to medium dry
Wines:	varietals, Terlano and Pinot Grigio (Italy), Tokay D'Alsace (France), Szurkebarat (Hungary), Rulander (Germany)
Comments:	distinctive, full-bodied wine, often lacking delicacy but mellows when mature — genuine member of the Pinot family — occasionally a little dull from low acidity — grown in France, Italy, Germany and Eastern Europe

∽

Grape Variety:	Sauvignon Blanc
Wine Colors:	pale yellow to gold

Nose:	clean, fruity aroma of blackcurrants, distinctive grassy bouquet, sometimes with a touch of wood
Taste:	often a pungent, spicy, almost vegetative taste — can be quite acidic at times — usually quite dry
Wines:	white wines of the Loire such as Sancerre, Pouilly-Fumé, the Fumé Blanc of California, also a part of the blend for Graves, Sauternes and Barsac in the Bordeaux region of France
Comments:	a very distinctive wine with a good long finish to it — somewhat coarse at times — often a crisp, acidic dry table wine — also one of the grapes blended to make the famous dessert wines of Sauternes and Barsac

ᗞ

Grape Variety:	Sylvaner
Wine Colors:	pale yellow / green to yellow
Nose:	bouquet and aroma similar to White Riesling (see) but not as pronounced
Taste:	similar to Riesling but more earthy, not as distinctive — lacks crispness — dry, to softly sweet — characteristic short finish (some exceptions) — is more distinctive when grown on chalky soils as in the Franconia district of Germany — medium dry to very sweet
Wines:	varietals — blended in many German white table wines, occasionally labelled simply "Riesling" in California
Comments:	best drunk young — a major variety in Germany (called Franken Riesling) — planted in Hungary, Yugoslavia, Czechoslovakia where it changes character significantly and is called Zirfandler — also grown in northern Italy and U.S.A.

Grape Variety: Trebbiano

Wine Colors: pale gold

Nose: saffron-like aroma, not an intense bouquet

Taste: faint taste of almonds — full-bodied, slightly astringent — dry to medium-sweet

Wines: White Chianti, a major part of the blend for Soave, also blended in Red Chianti

Comments: a major variety in Italy — grown in Southern France (Ugni Blanc) and now in small plantings in California — primary Cognac grape

ᔫ

Grape Variety: Walschriesling

Wine Colors: pale yellow / green to pale yellow

Nose: some very faint White Riesling (see) characteristics

Taste: light Riesling flavor with some bitterness in the aftertaste — characteristic short finish — dry to medium sweet

Wines: Rizling, varietals

Comments: not a true Riesling — perhaps a very distant cousin — widely grown in Eastern European countries and is labelled Riesling or Rizling — also known as Olasz Riesling, Laski Riesling, Grasavina or Italian Riesling

ᔫ

Grape Variety: White Riesling (Johannisberg Riesling)

Wine Colors: from very pale yellow / green to deep golds

Nose: fruity aroma (not grapey), clean flowery bouquet, very distinctive character

Taste: crisp fruity acidity — good long finish, some claim a taste of orange blossoms with a touch of cinnamon — dry to very sweet

Wines: the classic whites of Moselle, Rhine, varietals

Comments *THE* classic Riesling grape — light to medium body — from the very dry Alsatian varieties to the famous German dessert wines (Beerenauslese, Trockenbeerenauslese) — not usually high in alcohol (9-11%) — planted in almost every major wineland where it retains its basic varietal character — does better in cooler climates like Germany, Alsace and northern California — has many imposters like Grey Riesling, Missouri Riesling, Italian Riesling (Walschriesling) which are not true Rieslings at all — many good crosses of this grape such as the Sylvaner (Franken Riesling), Muller-Thurgau and the California cross, Emerald Riesling (with Muscadelle)

ა

VINIFERA RED VARIETIES

Grape Variety: Barbera
Wine Colors: light to deep ruby red
Nose: aroma of violets and cherries, distinctive berry-light bouquet
Taste: medium body, good acidity, prominent fruity flavor, dry
Wines: varietals primarily from Italy and California
Comments: best examples come from the Piedmont district in Italy — can be aged to a soft full wine in good years — good alcohol levels (12-13%) — a fruity wine maturing at 2-3 years of age

Grape Variety: Cabernet Franc

Wine Colors: dark red / purple to red / brown

Nose: less distinctive than the Cabernet Sauvignon (see) aroma, herbaceous bouquet

Taste: similar to Cabernet Sauvignon but not as distinctive, good acid content, astringent in youth, dry

Wines: Chinon, Bourqueil, Champigny of the Loire, many of the better rosés in that same French valley (e.g. Cabernet D'Anjou), a major grape used in Bordeaux especially for St. Emilion wines.

Comments: often stands in the shadow of the more reputed Cabernet Sauvignon — the finest rosés in the Loire come from this grape — grown very little outside of France — developing in northern Italy

✍

Grape Variety: Cabernet Sauvignon

Wine Colors: red / purple to mahogany (with age)

Nose: pungent aroma of blackcurrants and cedar — full, complex bouquet

Taste: warm, rich, often very tannic and harsh when young, a complex taste that improves with a touch of wood — dry — smooth, velvety texture at maturity with a long lasting flavor

Wines: many of the great Bordeaux Chateaux, Clarets, varietals

Comments: greatest red wine grape — does best in Bordeaux and California — also grown in Bulgaria, Italy, Spain, Yugoslavia, South Africa, Australia, New Zealand — varies in character somewhat from country to country but keeps its basic qualities and nature — very different wines due to much blending with other wines (Merlot as an example) — often tremendous ageing ability (decades)

✍

Grape Variety: Cinsault

Wine Colors: red/purple to brownish/red

Nose: light varietal aroma that develops a better, more complex bouquet with more spice to it with some wood and age

Taste: soft and full bodied — dry to medium dry — fine varietal character

Wines: important component in many wines from the South of France, like Chateauneuf-du-Pape, Minervois, Corbieres, Cotes du Rhone — the Hermitage of South Africa

Comments: a quality grape growing in importance in Southern France and South Africa (Hermitage) — also made into Rosés — good depth of color

✍

Grape Variety: Gamay

Wine Colors: light red/garnet to full red

Nose: fruity, aromatic aroma of raspberries

Taste: soft, fruity, refreshing taste — little or no bitterness or astringency — good acid balance — dry to medium dry

Wines: Beaujolais, rosés, varietals

Comments: light, fruity red wine — not high in alcohol or extract — doesn't age well — best when young and slightly chilled — the Gamay-Beaujolais vine is actually a member of the Pinot family — both it and the true Gamay (Gamay noir à jus blanc) are grown in the Beaujolais region of France, California and in Eastern Europe

Grape Variety: Grenache

Wine Colors: rosé to pale brownish / red

Nose: perfumed, somewhat spicy aroma, can be light to very pronounced bouquet, often wood aged

Taste: medium body, not usually tannic or acidic — fruity, grapey flavor — very dry to medium sweet

Wines: Tavel and Lirac rosés of France, varietals

Comments: often a major component in reds from Southern France and Spain — low pigment level is its major fault — native of Spain (Garnacha) used in many Rioja and Penedes wines — blended in Chateauneuf du Pape, Cotes du Rhone, Fitou, Corbieres, Minervois and the famous dessert wine, Banyuls — grown in France, Spain, North Africa, Australia and California where it does particularly well

***

Grape Variety: Merlot

Wine Colors: ruby red (occasionally slight orange reflections) to red / brown

Nose: fruity aroma of strawberries — herbaceous bouquet, good intensity

Taste: a soft round flavor, a little thin but it has individuality — dry with good acid balance

Wines: important blending grape in Bordeaux, varietals in Italy, California and Eastern Europe

Comments: does better in cooler climates — used in blends for its intense bouquet and softness — more important in the St. Emilion district of Bordeaux than in the Medoc — used widely in Pomerol — grown in France, California, Italy (5th most important vine) and most winelands in the world now

115

Grape Variety: Nebbiolo

Wine Colors: dark ruby red (with orange/yellow reflections)
to mahogany

Nose: aromatic, spicy bouquet of violets

Taste: some say of olives, and mushrooms (I suspect
they got too close to their antipasto) — full-bodied
— tannic in youth, dry, velvety-smooth when
mature — high in alcohol — good, long finish

Wines: Barolo, Barberesco, Gattinara, Carema,
Donnaz, Ghemme, Valtellina (the who's who
of Italian red wines), varietals

Comments: one of the truly superior red grapes — grown
primarily in Italy — produces classy, well-
balanced high quality red wines of great ageing
potential

෴

Grape Variety: Pinot Noir

Wine Color: medium to deep burgundy

Nose: pronounced but elusive bouquet, difficult to
describe in terms other than a *Pinot Noir* nose,
— an, over-ripe grape aroma, you'll have to
experience personally

Taste: elegant fruity quality — a distinctive pene-
trating flavor, not as tannic or dry as Cabernet
Sauvignon — great breed and power — silk-
like smoothness when fully mature — full-
bodied, dry

Comments: does not age as long as Cabernet Sauvignon
usually — 3-10 years depending on producer,
vintage and storage, with some rare exceptions
— grown in France, Germany (Spatburgunder),
Switzerland, Austria, Hungary, Rumania, Bulgaria, Italy, South Africa, Australia and
California where it is often lighter in
color and flavor

Grape Variety:	Pinotage
Wine Colors:	deep purple/red to garnet
Nose:	assertive, spicy aroma developing good complexity with age
Taste:	full bodied, big wine — good acid balance — fruity, Cinsault-like taste — some bitterness in the finish — medium to long flavor.
Wines:	Varietals
Comments:	a cross of Pinot Noir and Cinsault (called Hermitage in S. Africa — the Pinot element removes some of the "hot climate" characteristics — developed and primarily cultivated in South Africa — Australia, New Zealand and California are now experimenting with this variety too.

వ

Grape Variety:	Syrah
Wine Colors:	pale ruby to garnet and deep almost black/red to red/brown
Nose:	aroma of raspberries and pepper — distinctive bouquet at maturity, cedar-like, full
Taste:	very tannic in youth, matures slowly — truly a big wine, good acid balance, dry — mellows to a smooth full bodied rich wine at maturity
Wines:	Hermitage, Crozes Hermitage, Cornas, Cote Rotie, Shiraz of Australia, some true Syrah varietals in California (not Petite Sirah)
Comments:	rough, coarse, tannic in youth — one of the 13 grapes used in Chateauneuf du Pape

Grape Variety:	Zinfandel
Wine Colors:	pale yellow, to rosé, to deep ruby/red
Nose:	prominent fruity, berry-like aroma — some claim an aroma of bramble, wild blackberry — full distinctive, complex bouquet
Taste:	full flavored, can be very tannic, with the berry-like flavor — dry to very sweet
Wines:	Blanc de Noir Zinfandel (white), Zinfandel Rosé, red varietals — dessert wines
Comments:	native of Italy — known in Yugoslavia as Plavac or Plavina — California classic — Primitivo of Italy — varies widely in nature and quality in different regions — from the rare rich white to the fresh, dry and fragrant rosés, to light and big reds — better quality reds take ageing well — late harvested Zinfandel may carry on for decades — few, other than the lands mentioned cultivate this vine

࿘

EUROPEAN HYBRIDS

Grape Variety:	Seyval Blanc
Wine Colors:	pale yellow
Nose:	slight honey-like aroma, mildly fruity — very mild Labrusca — develops some bouquet
Taste:	delicate fruity taste — light to medium body — good acidity — medium to long finish — dry to medium sweet
Wines:	varietals, blending wine
Comments:	a golden yellow grape grown in France, Britain and eastern North America — a well balanced wine with a good future — Seyve-Villard (5276) cross of two Seibel hybrids

Grape Variety: Baco Noir

Wine Colors: red / purple

Nose: herbaceous aroma some say similar to some clarets — some Labrusca noticeable

Taste: rather neutral but a bit spicy — good alcohol and acid — full-bodied with a medium-long finish — very mild Labrusca character — dry

Wines: varietals, blending wine

Comments: usually develops good color depth — early ripening grape — grown in France and Eastern North America — Baco (No. 1) hybrid of Folle Blanche and Riparia

✍

Grape Variety: de Chaunac

Wine Colors: red / purple

Nose: fruity aroma similar at times to Gamay and some Pinots — mild Labrusca character — little bouquet development

Taste: some qualities of Gamay — light to medium-bodied — Labrusca mildly evident — medium to high acidity — dry

Wines: varietals, blending wine

Comments: early ripening grape — does not improve a great deal with age — Seibel 9549 hybrid — not very successful in France but now a major red variety in Canada and eastern United States

✍

Grape Variety: Marechal Foch

Wine Colors: red / purple to red / brown

Nose: herb-like aroma, very vinous — when well made can have little or no Labrusca evident — develops complexity with age

119

Taste: an earthy wine with a Burgundian/Rhone character — spicy, with full round body — good acid levels — dry but not austere

Wines: varietals, blending wine

Comments: good color depth — takes moderate ageing well — a Kuhlman 188.2 hybrid of Riparia/Rupestris by Goldriesling — very vigorous vine — grown in France, Eastern U.S.A. and Canada with a solid future ahead of it

✍

EARLY NORTH AMERICAN HYBRIDS

Grape Variety: Delaware

Wine Colors: pale to medium yellow

Nose: grapey aroma — distinctive spicy bouquet

Taste: delicate grapey flavor — slight mustiness (foxiness)

Wines: varietal

Comments: a pink grape — one of the finest early North American hybrid grapes — makes a fruity, soft wine with good body — pleasant without too much Labrusca foxiness — usually some residual sugar

✍

Grape Variety: Dutchess

Wine Colors: pale to medium yellow/green

Nose: spicy, flowery aroma, can have very little Labrusca noticeable

Taste: crisp in youth but develops a soft, round full body with a little time — very mild, pleasant Labrusca taste — pleasantly dry to medium dry

Wines: varietals, often a major part of Canadian and New York State Champagne-type wines

Comments: superior, distinctive early North American hybrid of Labrusca and Vinifera — late ripening white grape — grown only in eastern North America — a unique, very pleasant wine

ॐ

Grape Variety: Concord

Wine Colors: purple / red

Nose: musty (fox), grapey aroma, very persistent

Taste: heavy grapey flavor, overly prominent, lacks subtlety — quite acidic at times — dry to medium sweet

Wines: North American Kosher wines, Pop wines, varietals

Comments: typical native North American *slip-skin* grape — the backbone of eastern North American viticulture for generations — other native Vitis Labrusca varieties possess similar characteristics to lesser or greater degrees — foxiness caused by an ester (methyl / ethyl anthranilate) not present in Vinifera — characteristically low in sugar and high in acid

WINE AND FOOD
A Personal Viewpoint

I promised early in this book I would not burden you with my views of "which wines to serve with certain foods." I will not break that promise for there are sufficient books, booklets, magazines and pamphlets, from innumerable sources, that already contain an excess of such personal guidelines. However, I feel a necessity, an urgency really, to comment on the *relationship* of wine to food.

This may seem slightly out of context for a book such as this. Yet, we have spent many pages investigating *how* to taste and evaluate wines, the goal of which was to increase your appreciation of wine. But, there remains one vital thought I feel compelled to add.

Wine is quite capable of standing on its own merits!

I feel the need to make this point strongly because there seems to be a growing trend towards the idea that there is an *absolute necessity* to *marry* every wine with an appropriate food, to the extent a wine is often described in terms of what food it should be consumed with. Balderdash! Wine does not need food to be appreciated or improved upon. In fact, many of these unfortunate unions serve only to dilute the appreciation of wine.

This mandatory wine/food connection is becoming so widespread today that some wine journalists, educators and connoisseurs, when evaluating a wine, seem to feel their job is incomplete until they have matched that wine with some food or recipe. As a consequence there exists this attitude among some consumers that wine is not much more than a *compliment* to food. It is more. Indeed, it is more.

But please don't misinterpret these comments. I would not for a moment challenge the delightful inclusion of wine with meals, or with food at anytime, for that matter. They're natural partners. Some of these marriages produce veritable ambrosia. However, to appreciate the genuine pleasures of wine, food is not necessary and can be a considerable distraction, at times.

Including a truly **fine** or **great** wine with a meal, in my view, is like driving a Ferrari through rush hour traffic. Granted, if I must suffer the trauma of rush hour city traffic, sitting in a Ferrari is as desirable a way as there is to do it. But that's not the most exhilarating use to which this regal carriage can be put. And so it is for **fine** and **great** wines. They have so much more to offer than playing second fiddle to some Chef's concoction, as delightful as that concoction might be. More simple, or-dinary wines . . . pleasant wines that can be consumed with only pass-ing interest in their heritage, are the ideal meal mates.

To some this view may be somewhat unsettling, for the inclusion of food with the consumption of all alcoholic beverages is promoted these days in an attempt to counteract some of the problems associated with alcohol abuse. To satisfy any concern that this view of mine, if prolifer-ated, would somehow turn the clock back in this respect I must add that the most significant deterrent to abuse in knowledge. When some-one takes an interest in wine, pursuing it to greater depths of apprecia-tion and understanding, there is created an increased respect for this beverage and a decreased desire to abuse it . . . much more so than by simply ingesting some food with your wine. After all, most problem drinkers eat.

Education and **appreciation** are truly the roads to moderation!

The individual *personality* of a truly fine or great wine, its depth and complexity, all its intriguing attributes of smell, taste and feel — that's something that should be explored by your senses in an unadulterated fashion. In every sense of the word, **wine**, its appreciation and inclu-sion as part of life, is an **ART** . . . every bit as interesting, complex and rewarding as other art forms. It's not coincidence that throughout history the love of fine music, art and literature have been synonymous with the love of fine wines. And, as is the case for those other arts, the *art* of wine has its roots with the common man. It is not meant to be an elitist pursuit.

For those who may have grown up with wine, and who perhaps now take it almost for granted, giving it no more attention than their morn-ing coffee or tea, as well as for those who are just now making friends with the "product of the vine," there is ever so much to explore, so much to enjoy, so much to gain from wine . . . the most significant of which is the appreciation for the role wine can play in a moderate life.

Taste on!

Conclusion

I wish there was a clever and literate way to conclude this book. But, for the moment I have little I desire to add that would not repeat or confuse what has already been said.

So, if you find yourself reading this comment you'll know that the publisher had an extra blank page with nothing else to put on it.

Taste on!

Glossary Introduction

As intimated earlier the winetasters *lexicon* leaves a good deal to be desired. Everyone seems to have his own personal wine vocabulary, including yours truly. It's not that winetasters cannot communicate efficiently it's just that too many of us are wont to forget that words should be a means to accurately transmit thoughts to others, not solely to oneself.

What has developed over the past few decades is this generation's wine jargon. It sounds elegant, sophisticated and highly colorful but in truth confuses almost everyone but the user, and at times includes him. At most wine-related affairs these flamboyant, ambiguous wine terms fill the air like raindrops in a monsoon.

But, I'm happy to see, perhaps from sheer necessity alone, that a number of wine words are becoming more universally understood in wine circles. Even the wine scientist and the connoisseur are more frequently talking about the same things these days when they use certain words. Mind you, I don't mean to create any false hopes for a final linguistic fusion. The gap between the usage of accurate and obscure wine words remains distinctly chasmic.

And, once more I must explain that I have not taken it upon myself to try to resolve the differences in the following Glossary. Hopefully these few pages will shed a bit of light on the matter. If it accomplishes that I'll consider it a worthwhile exercise. If it further confuses the issue – my apologies.

But in all fairness, there is a decided tendency in virtually every field of endeavour to condense what is most accurately described by several words down to a single, hopefully succinct term. As is so often the case that selected word falls short in some respects or leaves itself open for rather liberal interpretations. Much of the current wine jargon merely echoes this pattern.

For all winetasters – scientists, professionals, connoisseurs, buffs and yes, most importantly, for everyday wine consumers – there is need to simplify and universalize wine language. This is not an attempt to start a crusade or movement rather, simply to raise somewhat the conscious need to be more specific in the way we describe the grandest beverage of all.

Glossary

ACETIC — the taste and odor of *vinegar* – caused by acetic acid and ethyl acetate – a negative factor – from several causes – excessive air contact a major culprit.

ACID — (see page 74) referring to desirable, pleasant fruit acids creating the *tart*, *crispness* of a wine – an essential component in sound wines – major contributor to a wine's *bouquet* development.

AFTERTASTE — the lingering *flavor* (see) experienced after swallowing some wine – quality wines have a balanced, pleasant *length* of flavor while ordinary wines are often characterized by a short *finish* – if too long it can also be a fault.

ALCOHOL — a basic wine component ranging from 7-20% – several types are found in wine, the major one being *ethyl* alcohol – perceptible in the nose, in a tactile sense (see **HOT**) and by taste *(sweetish)* – accounts for much of a wine's *body* – a factor that should be balanced for the type of wine.

AROMA – a wine odor originating with the *fruit*, the grape itself – varies in nature according to grape variety – declines with age.

ASTRINGENCY – a *tactile* (touch) stimulation originating with the wine's tannins – described as harsh, rough, coarse – often leaves a *gritty* feeling on the teeth and lips – as the wine ages the tannins should decrease leaving a *smooth* wine some refer to as soft and velvety.

BAKED – caramel-like odor from wines that literally have been heated – Madeira, Marsala and some sherry-like dessert wines possess this nature – more loosely applied to table wines from hotter climates with a dried, *raisiny* character.

BALANCE –the pleasing *harmony* of a wine's taste, olfactory and tactile elements.

BIG – a rather ambiguous term used to describe wines with a *healthy* compliment of various wine constituents like extract, alcohol, tannins, acids, etc.

BITE – suggests a strong measure of acidity – more common to youthful wines.

BITTERNESS – one of the four *true taste* stimulations – best detected on the rear surface of the tongue – can have more than one source – youthful bitterness should disappear with age – a degree of bitterness may characterize some wines for their lifespan – some tasters accustomed to it defend wines with a touch of bitterness – most significant question to ask . . . is the bitterness offensive?

BODY – a *tactile* sensation – *texture* and *consistency* are synonyms – created primarily by the alcohol content – glycerine, residual sugars, *extract* and *tannins* also play a role – opposite of full-bodied is *thin*.

BOUQUET – odors created from the *fermentation* process and from subsequent wood and bottle *ageing* – technically, the slow oxidation of the wine's fruit acids, esters and alcohols – a complex odor structure that should grow with proper ageing.

127

BREED – a vague term supposedly referring to the factors like superior grape variety, ideal soil and climate condition, etc., which account for a quality wine – we could do well without the word.

BRIGHT (Brilliant) – total lack of observable suspended material affecting the clarity of a wine – *limpid*, a synonym.

CARAMEL(IZED) – toffee-like odor of wines that have been heated or have had *cooked* musts added to them; in wines like Madeira, Marsala, some types of Sherries and some sherry-like dessert wines.

CHARACTER – ambiguous reference to quality either of specific components or to the wine in general terms – like the word *personality*, what is meaningful is *what* type not *how* much.

CHARACTERISTIC – a good substitute word when you're not certain of the appropriate specific term – broadly meant to identify a certain nature related to such things as grape variety, region, district or vintage.

CLEAN – freedom from *off* odors and tastes – a basic starting point for wine quality – both ordinary and *great* wines should be clean.

CLEAR – not *crystal* clarity – an acceptable level, with perhaps some discernable suspended particles.

CLOUDY – abundant suspended particles (*colloidal*) sufficient to seriously impair the clarity of the wine

CLOYING – an excessive, lingering, *flabby*, sweetness – sometimes accompanied by low acidity.

COARSE – primarily a reference to the *harshness* caused by the combination of too much acidity and bitterness – not the roughness of a young wine, rather that of a poorly made one with little hope of improvement.

COMPLEXITY – the existence of numerous odor components in the *nose and taste* of a wine supposedly indicating quality grapes, proper processing and perceptible wood ageing.

CORKED (Corky) – musty odor from a cork that has been affected by bacteria or. chemicals used in processing the corks – the musty odor eventually infects the wine – easily identified.

DELICATE – badly misused term – a polite way of expressing a deficiency.

DRY – the absence of sweetness – usually below 1% residual sugar.

DULL – (a) see CLOUDY (b) low acidy.

DUMB – an *educated* guess which defines a young, undeveloped wine that will blossom forth with quality when it matures – also descriptive of some users of this word when such predictions are unfounded.

EARTHY – *in-mouth* odor supposedly indicative of certain soils - as many descriptions for this word as there are tasters.

ELEGANT – more suited to the fashion trade than to wine.

EXTRACT – dissolved wine solids (minus sugar) - contributor to the body of a wine.

FINE – overused commercial wine term - properly applied it indicates a quality level just above "vin ordinaire", below "great".

FINESSE – non-specific term for wine.

FINISH – see AFTERTASTE.

FLAT – (a) low acidy, (b) a sparkling wine that has lost its bubbles.

FLAVOR – a stimulation perceived by the combined abilities of your nose and taste receptors -"in-mouth odors" as some express it - these two sensory devices produce a *synergistic* response identifying a combination of *olfactory* and *true taste* stimulations as a single element, called **flavor** - degrees of flavor are often determined by the length of that flavor, expressed as *finish* or *aftertaste* (see).

FLINTY – find another word for what you think this means.

FLOWERY – a *floral-like* fragrance similar to that of certain flowers -detected in the *nose* of the wine.

FOXY – a *wet-fur*, *musky-like* odor and taste exhibited by some native North American species of grapes, primarily *Vitis Labrusca* technically, created by methyl and ethyl anthranilate - these chemical substances are not found in *Vitis Vinifera* (European grapes) - a non-qualitative factor unless it is too persistent and exaggerated.

FRAGRANT – it sounds like too nice a wine-word to give up but I don't know what it means specifically.

FRESH – broad terminology for wines exhibiting a *youthful* nature.

FRUITY – pleasant, aromatic taste and smell of fresh grapes - usually associated with good levels of fruit acids and sugars.

FULL-BODIED –see BODY - most appropriate to dessert wines with higher sugar, glycerine, extract and alcohol content.

GRAPEY – heavy grape aroma originating with varities like the Muscat family, Labrusca's, etc.

GREEN – the odor and taste from unripe grapes when made into wine -high malic acid a major factor.

HARD – (HARSH) used to describe youthful tannic state of a wine, with additional excesses in acid occasionally accompanied by low alcohol - time should cure the condition.

HARMONY – see BALANCE

HAZY – not as serious as **Cloudy** (see) but sufficient suspended material to detract from the wine's appearance.

HEAVY – *full-bodied* (see) taken to excess.

HERBACEOUS – **natural** wine odors reminiscent of herbs - not from the addition of botanicals such as with Vermouths, etc.

HONEYED – as close as you can get to describing an odor given off by some well-aged, sweet wines like Sauternes, Beerenauslese, Trockenbeerenauslese and Tokaji.

HOT – mild *pain* sensation from high alcohol content - also described as *fiery*.

LIGHT – deficiency of elements that create *body* - not unpleasant - can contribute to *balance* in a wine with low alcohol.

MADERIZED – most often a reference to white wines that, due to improper storage, show the signs of oxidation in taste and color - see **BAKED** - will exhibit gold, amber and brown color tinges.

MALIC ACID –the major organic acid of unripe grapes - resembles the acidic taste in green apples - as grapes ripen malic acid decreases -bacteria in wine can transform it to softer lactic acid (malo-lactic fermentation).

MELLOW – another equivocal wine term - has traditionally meant a *softness* in the wine - a term being used more and more to describe red wine with a touch of residual sugar.

METALLIC – rarely related to actual metals in wine but extreme rarities of iron and copper excesses can create this sensation - more often it refers to a *metallic-like* sensation of low alcohol, high acid dry whites - some highly astringent reds can also create this sensation.

MOLDY – an odor of mold infecting the wine - originating from poorly maintained containers that have had mold growing in them - can also come from grapes that have been affected by the non-beneficial mold called *pourriture grise.*

MOUSY – an *acetic acid-like* odor and taste caused by bacteria - most often occurs in late-harvested grapes that were low in organic acids.

MUSKY – peculiar, characteristic odor exhibited in wines from the Muscat family retaining some sugar.

MUST – unfermented grape juice and/or mash.

MUSTY – dubious wine term.

NEUTRAL – a wine exhibiting low intensity in olfactory, tactile and taste sensations - little to cause offense, little to make it memorable.

NOBLE – aristocratic but foggy term supposedly applied to superior wines.

NOSE – broad term describing the collective enological elements assessed by the olfactory organ of your proboscis - (English translation). . . general wine odors.

NUTTY – pungent, nut-like odor and taste - usually found in Amontillado-type Sherries and Tawny Ports - probably from wood and acetaldehydes.

OFF – seriously negative odor or taste - opposite of *clean.*

OLFACTORY – the sense of smell - see page

ORGANOLEPTIC – in this case, a sensory evaluation of wine - more than a casual inspection is intimated.

OXIDIZED – exposure to too much air - may result from advanced age or from poor handling, processing or storage - basically you are smelling a substance called acetaldehyde.

POOR – as a general quality level for wine this word identifies wines with little merit or distinction but are certainly drinkable - a stage below "vin ordinaires."

PRICKED – an awkward expression that is supposed to define a wine with excessive *volatile* acidity (vinegar) but may still be in the drinkable stage.

PUNGENT – vague wine term to be used at your own risk.

RAISINY – a wine odor created by using grapes that are partially or completely dried - also evident to a lesser degree in some wines produced from grapes grown in hot climates.

RIPE – the personal peak for an individual wine - a fully mature wine before its decline - it remains in this state for various lengths of time, unique to each wine.

ROUGH – another term to describe the astringent tactile stimulation when it is excessive.

RUBBERY – a negative, self descriptive odor of complex chemical origin.

SALTY – *true taste* stimulation - the normal concentrations of sodium in wines are below human sensory thresholds - occasionally some tasters claim to sense a salty tang in some Manzanilla and old, dry Flor Sherries - perceptible to some tasters when ion exchange resins are poorly applied to preserve some wines.

SAUERKRAUT – an excess of Lactic acid - most often from too strong a malo-lactic fermentation.

SHARP – well-known wine educator and author *(I couldn't let it go by)* see **TART**.

SMOKEY – uncertain significance.

SMOOTH – opposite to ASTRINGENT, HARSH, ROUGH - a *silk-like* texture.

SOFT – used to describe too many characteristics.

SORBIC ACID – acid added to wine as a preservative - limited applications - can sometimes be detected by a *geranium-like* odor.

SOUR – laboratory language for the true acid (not acetic acid) taste -see **TART** and **ACID**.

SPICY – the *spice-like* odor and taste of some grape varieties - the outstanding example is the Gewurtztraminer.

STEMMY (Stalky) – a green, wet, wood-like odor and taste usually caused by improper removal of grape stems from the *must*.

SULPHUR – almost a necessity in the wine industry - small amounts are naturally produced in wine - added in various forms at different stages of processing - acts as a sterilising agent, killing bacteria and germs without destroying yeast cells - separates into *free* and *chemically bound* sulphur - *free* is what can be detected on the *nose*, when above 50 parts per million.

SWEET – a *true taste* stimulation originating from several wine sources, primarily natural sugars (fructose, sucrose and glucose) - also capable of demonstrating a mild sweetness are glycerine, alcohol and some strains of yeast - sweetness is neither an absolute *positive* or *negative* factor - needs to be balanced with other elements like acid and alcohol.

TANNIN – an organic element found in the skins, stalks and pips of grapes - it can also be extracted from wooden barrels during ageing -creates *astringent* (see) feeling - tactile sense not a taste - necessary for beneficial ageing of wine - most prominent in young red wines, as white wines are generally fermented off their skins - percipitates out as a deposit during the ageing process.

TART – too much acid without sufficient sugar to balance it out - may decrease with some ageing.

TARTARIC ACID – a major wine acid - largely responsible for the crisp, acidic tastes in wine with sufficient quantities - can also create those tartrate crystals spoken of on page

THIN – opposite of **FULL-BODIED** (see) - often described in terms of being *watery*.

THRESHOLD – a point beyond which you lose the ability to sense tactile, olfactory or taste stimulations - with exercise improvements can be made.

VELVET(Y) – texture or tactile description - use carefully as it can change character according to each user.

VINEGAR – acetic acid and ethyl acetate - see **ACETIC** -detectable by taste and smell.

VINUOUS – a simple, detectable *winey* nature minus the distinction of varietal qualities - see **NEUTRAL**.

WATERY – see **THIN**

WOODY – odor and taste of wood extracted from barrel ageing (usually oak) - if excessive in reds it can be a fault - desirable in only a few whites.

YEASTY – odor of fermenting or fermented yeasts - should disappear within months following a wine's primary fermentation.

Bibliography

In a work such as this it is not uncommon to be presented in the latter pages with a long list of reference material the author employed to assist and inspire him in his endeavours. And it only seems correct and fitting that these sources receive due credit.

But at the risk of appearing impudent I'll not present such a list for *Winetasters Secrets.* This is not due to any lack of appreciation for those wine authors whose works I have read with respect and admiration, but because the list is so long. At this point it would be almost impossible for me to determine which bit of information and data came from which source.

Perhaps it is sufficient for me to admit that little in this book is original. It is founded on works, judgments, and opinions of innumerable winelovers, many who penned their experiences and thoughts long before I came to be.

What more can I say!

Index

W

XYZ

Photography and Graphics Acknowledgments

Chapter Page Graphics   Kevin Thorogood
Graphics – pages 24 & 28   Walter Graham
Photographs
Pages 21, 30, 34, 37, 43   Lovello
Page 50   Courtesy Bouchard Pere et Fils
Page 52   Lovello
Page 60   Courtesy Robert Mondavi Wines
Page 64   Lovello
Page 67   Courtesy Sebastiani Wines,
                                            California
Page 68   Courtesy Bouchard Pere et Fils
Page 76   Courtesy Gallo Wines
Page 80   Courtesy Heidsieck Champagne
Page 84   Courtesy Taittinger Champagne
Page 87   Lovello (top)
Page 100   Courtesy Beaulieu Vineyards,
                                            California